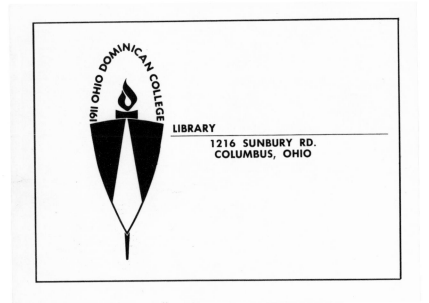

FAERIES

Described and Illustrated by
Brian Froud and Alan Lee

Edited and Designed by David Larkin

Harry N. Abrams, Inc. Publishers, New York
Souvenir Press
Peacock Press / Bantam Books, Toronto, New York, London
Pan Books, London and Sydney.

*We are most grateful to the publishers and authors who have
kindly allowed us to use their material:*

Colin Smythe Limited for extracts from *The Middle Kingdom* by
Dermot Mac Manus.

The Folklore Society for an extract from
Somerset Folklore Country Series VIII by Ruth L. Tongue.

EP Publishing Limited for extracts from *British Goblins* by
Wirt Sikes (originally published by Sampson Low, Marston,
Searle & Rivington – 1880).

Samuel Weiser, Inc. for extracts from *The Coming of the Fairies*
by Arthur Conan Doyle.

Theosophical Publishing House Ltd for extracts from *Fairies
at Work and at Play* by Geoffrey Hodson.

We are also indebted to Sarah Teale for her invaluable editorial
assistance and advice in the preparation of this book.

Library of Congress Catalogue Card Number:
78–60699
Published in 1978 by Harry N. Abrams, Inc., New
York: ISBN 0–8109–0901–4
First British edition published in 1978 by Souvenir
Press Ltd., in association with Pictorial Presentations
Ltd., 43 Great Russell Street, London WC1B 3PA:
ISBN 0 285 62359 1
Published in 1979 by Peacock Press/Bantam Books,
New York: ISBN 0–553–01159–6
Published in 1979 by Pan Books Ltd., 18-21 Cavaye
Place, London SW10 9PG: ISBN 0 330 257560

Color reproduction by Carlton Repro International Ltd,
a division of Sir Joseph Causton & Sons Ltd, London and Eastleigh.

A note on the
use of the word
F·A·E·R·IE

The words 'fey' and 'faerie' come from the French
and started to replace the Old English 'elf' during the
Tudor period. Spenser and Shakespeare popularised
the change. 'Elfland' and 'Faerieland', 'Elf' and
'Faerie' were and are still interchangeable words.
The spellings of 'faerie' are numerous: fayerye, fairye,
fayre, faerie, faery, fairy. In this book Faerie refers to
the world of Faerie as an entity (noun), as a
geographical location, as a general name for its
inhabitants (faerie, faeries) and as an adjective to
describe its attributes, e.g., faerie music. Fairy
(fairies) is applied to a particular, diminutive,
generally female species of Faerie; or when the
spelling is common usage, e.g. fairy Tool, a hill,
Yellow Fairy Club, a toadstool; or if used in a source
quotation.

A note on terminology

Nomenclature is difficult in Faerie. The same faerie
species may have various names according to the
region. The denizens of Faerie are so varied that in the
past some have been wrongly or carelessly
categorized. One species shades into the next, so it is
difficult to state precisely where a Bogie ends and a
Bogle begins. And what of the shape of shifting
faeries? In one form they may be in one category and
in another form a quite different one. Hence no
sensible rules apply to terminology or, indeed, any
other aspect of Faerie – it is a law unto itself. We shall
do the best we can to clarify with the facts available.

The pronunciation of many of the names of specific
faerie individuals or tribes may be difficult. For
purposes of clarity, however, we have given where
possible approximate pronunciation equivalents
after proper names.

Foreword — By Way of Introduction

We say "by way of" because there really is no introduction to the world of Faerie. That is, no one can introduce you to faeries. (This is an old-fashioned idea, probably rooted in the wealth of questionable fiction about these ubiquitous creatures).

The fact is, they will either accept you as a part of their world, or they won't. It's up to them. Sometimes indeed, a totally unwilling human will nevertheless become captive (i.e. captivated) — taken by Faerie for their own purposes. Sometimes no amount of mooning around in misty forest glades or communing with nature at the bottom of the garden (erroneously said to be a favourite haunt of faeries) will bring about anything other than a general sense of damp.

Our own personal experience with faeries is complicated. This is necessarily so with creatures of such varied and ever-changing character. In an effort to bring some order, at least, to a controversial subject, we have explored legend, myth, folklore, faerielore and even outright fantasy. It has been necessary to sift down the mass of material thus accumulated to practical dimensions. Our book therefore is divided up into various categories of faerie (where possible) and into various categories of faerie experience.

And here we must make one thing very clear. The real faerie experience is very different from the general view of faerie built up by clouds of sentimental fiction with legions of inevitable happily-ever-after endings. The world of "Once Upon a Time —", delightful as it is and highly as we value it, is not the real world of Faerie. Faerie represents Power, magical power, incomprehensible to humans, and hence, inimical. It must always be remembered that though the world of Faerie is to a large extent dependent on humans, faeries are alien creatures with values and ethics far removed from mankind: they do not think, and most notably, they do not *feel*, the way that humans do.

This is precisely the core of much of their envy of mortals and the source of a good deal of the trouble they cause, for faeries are themselves creatures of the raw stuff of life and are ceaselessly attracted to all forms of creativity and particularly to moments of high emotion in which they seek to be participants. Lovers, poets, artists, writers, sculptors, weavers, musicians and the like — all the arts, indeed, acknowledge a debt to an unidentifiable, invisible, capricious, sensitive, delicate, elusive and powerful force which is called "inspiration", or "Muse" and is generally irresistible when present. It is no coincidence that these are also the chief characteristics of Faerie. Hence Faerie should be held as infinitely valuable.

Faerie is a world of dark enchantments, of captivating beauty, of enormous ugliness, of callous superficiality, of humour, mischief, joy and inspiration, of terror, laughter, love and tragedy. It is far richer than fiction would generally lead one to believe and, beyond that, it is a world to enter with extreme caution, for of all things that faeries resent the most it is curious humans blundering about their private domains like so many ill-mannered tourists. So go softly — where the rewards are enchanting, the dangers are real.

But the time is getting short for the taking of such delicious risks — faerie contact with humans, dependent as it is on the natural world of humans, is shrinking with our own shrinking habitat. It is time — and beyond — to distinguish the accumulated superstitions and conjectural fictions about Faerie from its reality, to study the world of Faerie with, we hope, kindly objectivity and a proper enjoyment of its true value to man.

Betty Ballantine

The myths and legends about Faerie are many and diverse, and often contradictory. Only one thing is certain – that nothing is certain. All things are possible in the land of Faerie.

Faerie Origins:
The mystery of Faerie has been, from the earliest times, a subject of human speculation. What are faeries? Where did they come from?

Norse mythology relates how the maggots emerging from the corpse of the giant Ymir transformed themselves into the Light Elves and the Dark Elves. Light elves, living in the air, are benign, happy creatures, but the dark elves, whose domains are the underground regions, are swarthy, evil and blighting.

The Icelandic version, on the other hand, states that Eve was washing all her children by the river when God spoke to her. In her awe and fear she hid those children she had not already washed. God asked if all her children were there and she replied that they were. He then declared that those she had hidden from him would be hidden from man. These hidden children became the elves or faeries and were known as Huldre Folk in the Scandinavian countries. Huldre girls are exceptionally beautiful, but with long cowstails; or else they are hollow behind, presenting only a beautiful front. Thus they fulfil the deception of their origin.

Elsewhere faeries are believed to be fallen angels; or the heathen dead, not good enough for Heaven, but not evil enough to find a place in Hell – compelled to live forever 'in between' in the twilight regions, the Middle Kingdom. In Devon for instance pixies are considered to be the souls of unbaptised children. However, these beliefs stem only from the advent of Christianity, baptism being unknown prior to that time, and hence cannot be regarded as reliable. Faerie is very ancient and predates Christianity by several millenia. Moreover it exists, and has existed, in varying forms, in many countries all over the world.

The Realm of Faerie

Where is 'Faerieland'? Its position is elusive. It is sometimes just over the horizon and sometimes beneath our feet. Yet there have been periods when faerieland was thought to be an actual geographical area, although even this has tended to shift. For instance, the Welsh first thought it was to the North of their mountainous land, and then in the mysterious, rocky and misty west peninsular of Pembrokeshire. Later it moved to an island lying in the Irish Channel off the Pembrokeshire coast. It was seen sometimes by sailors, and even landed on, but would then disconcertingly disappear. Nevertheless, its faerie inhabitants were said to be frequent visitors to the markets of Laugharne and Milford Haven. The Irish called the phantom isle Hy Breasail and, for them, it lay to the West. To Britons it was the Isle of Man that was the faerie isle. The Isle of Man is a rich source of faerie lore.

Avalon is probably the most famous of faerie islands. The legendary King Arthur, described by the XVth century poet Lydgate as a 'King y-crowned in Fairye', was brought here mortally wounded to be tended by four faerie queens. Arthur is believed still to lie with his knights, in the heart of a faerie hill, in a deep sleep from which he will awake in our hour of need again to rule over this land.

Faerie can reveal itself, bright and glittering without warning, anywhere and just as suddenly disappear. Its frontiers of twilight, mists and fancy are all around us and, like a tide running out, can momentarily reveal Faerie before flowing back to conceal it again. The inhabitants of faerieland can be divided into various different species according to habitat. In addition to the solitary-living faeries, there are many rural elf types who make their homes in the forests (or sometimes, more specifically, 'adopt' a tree to such an extent that the faerie and the tree become more or less synonymous), fields, hills and mountain caves. There are those that live on faerie islands or in countries under the oceans while there are also water faeries inhabiting the seas, lakes and rivers. Finally there are the domestic and house-spirits (brownies and so forth).

Amongst the various species, life-styles vary considerably between the small family units, the hierarchically-organised communities (often inhabiting hollow hills) and the solitary independent faeries such as the Leprechauns.

Each hill has
its own King
and Queen,
but they
usually
owe fealty
to a
'High King'

The best known of
these, the 'Oberon' of
mediæval Romance owes
his low stature to a curse
placed on him at his
baptism

HOLLOW HILLS

Ancient earthworks, forts and barrows are the traditional home of faeries. The Gaelic for faerie is Sidhe (Shee) meaning people of the hills. At night faerie hills are often seen ablaze with myriad sparkling lights. Sometimes the hill may raise itself up on pillars to reveal the brilliant lights of Faerie which gradually move off in procession towards another hill. Lammas Tide (August 7) is the traditional time for this. Hollantide (November 11) is, however, the time when Hillmen or Hogmen, the most feared of Manx Faerie people, choose to move their abode. One does not venture abroad on the night of November 11 if one is wise. Hogmen use well trodden paths and ways, usually running in straight lines between faerie hills; centuries of moving in this way has led to an invisible faerie cats-cradle crossing the whole country. Over the millenia, a residual concentration of power has accumulated at the junctions, or crossways, of these paths, and these junctions are close to many historically sacred human gathering places.

It is definitely not recommended that faerie hills (or other habitat) be invaded by trespassers. But there is nothing to be said against discreet observation, and a friendly watcher may be rewarded. If, however, the faeries seem reluctant to emerge from their hill, the entrance may be discovered by walking nine times around the hill at full moon. The entry way will then be revealed. For those not brave enough actually to enter the faeries home, an ear pressed close to the ground may be rewarded by the sounds of faerie revels.

Besides being used for living in, the hollow hills are hiding places for gold, and are also often used as faerie burial places. We already know about King Arthur. Another king, King Sil, sits in his golden armour on his horse, deep inside Silbury Hill, Wiltshire.

A similar story surrounds the Hill of the Goblins, Bryn yr Ellyllon, near Mold, Clyd Flint; it is haunted by a figure in gold armour. Excavations as recent as 1833 did in fact reveal a skeleton with a gold corselet.

Faeries go to great pains to protect their homes and their gold. Treasure seekers digging into faerie hills are warned by strange voices, baleful sounds and wild storms. Should these warnings be ignored, ill luck, disaster and even death will be the only reward. The Reverend F. Warne relates in 'Proceeding', 1854, how some men, eager to find treasure in a hill known as Castle Neroche in Somerset, 'violated the sanctity of this mysterious hill. But before they had found a single coin they were seized with a panic fear, and renounced their presumptuous enterprises, and wonderful and awful to relate, within one month of the commencement of their enterprise, some by accident, some by sudden death, and some by violent fevers, all paid with their lives.'

Reported in the 'Old Lore Miscellany' of July, 1911, is an account of an Orkney farmer, warned by a Trow not to dig in a mound in his field on pain of losing six cows and 'six funerals from the house, fellow', who nevertheless continued his depredations and lost both cattle and family.

Clearly one cannot idly invade or desecrate the chosen habitat of faeries. Ill-advised is he who elects to build on faerie terrain for the little people are perfectly capable of moving houses, churches and even castles if they object to their location. Houses built imprudently across a faerie path suffer from disturbance. One such afflicted house build in Ireland had an outside corner that was just overlapping a faerie way. At night the house was filled with noise and shook and seemed to be in danger of falling down. It was not until the offending corner was trimmed off that peace came to the house. In similar cases the problem has been solved to some extent by leaving the front and back doors open at night to allow the faeries free passage. Despite this rather chilly solution many small cottages in Ireland, as a precaution against this type of disturbance, have their front and back doors opposite each other.

Witches are frequent visitors to faerie huts – one of the many accusations levelled at them during the witch trials in the seventeenth century. Isobel Gowdie confessed in 1662 that she got 'meat there from the Qwein of Faerie, more than I could eat'

The connection between Glastonbury tor and
Gwyn ap-Nudd, along with its better known
associations with King Arthur's Avalon is
made more interesting still by the
fact that the Holy Tree which
allegedly grew from the staff of
Joseph of Aramathea was a thorn.
These are sacred to Faerie.

Thorn trees on a hill are a strong indication that faeries might abide there.

Faerie musicians have a magical skill, and many
songs and airs which today are widely known in the
human world have their origins in Faerie. The
Londonderry air is one such tune. Faeries are
passionately fond of music and outstanding human
musicians are at risk of being lured into the land of
Faerie for the sake of their talent.

Faerie melodies are known to be beautiful and
plaintive yet wild and capricious and they have a fatal
charm for mortal ears. A wistful faerie air may lull the
listener into a fatal sleep while, at best, he might
become drawn into a melancholic forgetfulness,
hearing forever the vague, yearning music, a constant
reminder of the unattainable. Morgan Gwilym, who
saw the faeries and heard their music dying away was
only able (fortunately for him) to recall the final
strains which, he said, sounded like this:

Faeries play a variety of musical instruments; fiddles harps, tambourines cymbals and the jews harp.

Akin to their passion for music, faeries good or evil adore to dance. The commonest form is a sort of circular dance in which the little people when they have no partners, leap and twist alone in a wild reel. Human beings who join them in their revels should beware for it can lead to a wasting sickness...

THE LEGEND OF KNOCKGRAFTON

There is an Irish faerie legend which tells of an unfortunate humpback called Lusmore who lived in a fertile glen at the foot of the gloomy Galtee mountains. T. Crofton Croker in his '*Fairy Legends and Traditions of the South of Ireland*' tells us that poor Lusmore (so called because he always wore a sprig of Lusmore or foxglove in his little straw hat) suffered twofold from his deformity as the country people were somewhat frightened of his unnatural appearance and shunned him. Lusmore's hump was gigantic, 'he looked just as if his body had been rolled up and placed on his shoulders and his head was pressed down with the weight so much that his chin, when he was sitting, used to rest on his knees for support.' Some ignorant locals even made up strange stories about him although this was probably also out of envy as Lusmore was a talented craftsman, plaiting straw and rushes into fine hats and baskets which invariably fetched a better price than those made by others.

One evening however as Lusmore was returning home from the pretty town of Cahir, he sat down a moment to rest his weary limbs by the old moat of Knockgrafton. Presently he heard beautiful yet unearthly music coming from the moat. The melody was so captivating that Lusmore listened intently until he became weary of the repetition of the tune. After a while there was a pause and Lusmore took up the song himself, raising it higher, and then went on singing with the voices inside the moat. The faeries were delighted with this variation in their melody and 'with instant resolve, it was determined to bring the mortal among them, whose musical skill so far exceeded theirs, and little Lusmore was conveyed into their company with the eddying speed of a whirlwind.' The happy faeries paid just tribute to Lusmore's talent, placing him above all their musicians and they feted him and honored him 'as if he had been the first man in the land'.

Presently Lusmore noticed a great consultation going on and was somewhat alarmed until one faerie stepped out from the rest and said:

> 'Lusmore! Lusmore!
> Doubt not, nor deplore,
> For the hump which you bore
> On your back is no more;
> Look down on the floor,
> And view it, Lusmore!'

Lusmore felt an unaccustomed lightness on his shoulders and was so thrilled 'he could have bounded at one jump over the moon.' He looked around with wonderment, able to lift up his head for the first time and everything appeared more and more beautiful. 'Overpowered at beholding such a resplendent scene, his head grew dizzy, and his eyesight became dim.' At last he fell into a sound sleep, and when he awoke, wonder of wonders, he was like a different man. Dressed in a brand new suit, which must have come from the faeries, he saw himself now to have become 'a well-shaped dapper little fellow'.

Not long after, when the story of Lusmore's hump was well-known around the countryside, an old woman came to his home to ask details of his 'cure' for the son of an acquaintance who was a humpback. Lusmore was a good-natured fellow and willingly described what had happened. The woman thanked him kindly and went home. She told her friend what Lusmore had said and they journeyed across the country with the humpback to the old moat of Knockgrafton. Now the humpback, Jack Madden was his name, was 'a peevish and cunning creature from his birth'. When he heard the faerie music he was in such a hurry to get rid of his hump that he never thought of waiting for an appropriate moment to sing a variation, or indeed that he should mind the quality of his singing. So he just broke into the faeries' singing, bawling out his words 'thinking that if one day was good, two were better; and that if Lusmore had one new suit of clothes given him, he should have two.'

The faeries were beside themselves with anger at this intrusion, whisked Jack Madden into the moat with tremendous force and surrounded him screeching and yelling. One stepped out of the crowd and said:

> 'Jack Madden, Jack Madden!
> Your words came so bad in
> The tune we felt glad in;-
> This castle you're had in,
> That your life we may sadden;
> Here's two humps for Jack Madden!'

and with that 'twenty of the strongest faeries brought Lusmore's hump, and put it down upon poor Jack's back, over his own, where it became fixed as firmly as if it was nailed on with twelve-penny nails, by the best carpenter that ever drove one'.

The faeries then kicked the unfortunate fellow out of their castle and he was found in the morning half dead, with the double hump on his shoulders, by the two women. Needless to say the unlucky Jack Madden did not survive long, what with the journey home and the tremendous weight on his shoulders, and he died soon after.

FAERIE RINGS

Faeries often dance in circles in the grass which are called faerie rings and this spells danger for the human passerby. The wild enchantment of the faerie music can lead him inexorably towards the ring which, like a faerie kiss or faerie food and drink, can lead to captivity for ever in the world of Faerie. If a human steps into the ring he is compelled to join the faeries in their wild prancing. The dance might seem to last only minutes, or an hour or two, or even at most a whole night but in fact the normal duration would be seven years by our time and sometimes longer. The unfortunate captive can be rescued by a friend who, with others holding his coat-tails, follows the faerie music, reaches into the ring (keeping one foot firmly outside) and pulls the dancer out.

There is the tale of a certain shepherd, Tudur of Llangollen, who came across a troop of faeries dancing to the music of a tiny fiddler. Tudur tried to resist the enchanting strains but finally, throwing his cap in the air and shouting: 'Now for it then, play away old devil' he joined in.

Immediately a pair of horns appeared on the fiddler's head and a tail sprouted from beneath his coat. The dancing sprites turned into goats, dogs, cats and foxes and they and Tudur span around in a dizzying frenzy. This lasted until the following day when Tudur was rescued by his master who found him, apparently alone, dancing like a madman. Some pious words broke the charm and Tudur was restored to his home.

The different time span in Faerie most certainly inspired many tales in popular literature, the best known of which is probably that of Rip Van Winkle by Washington Irving.

One legend tells of a young man called Shon ap Shenkin who, a fine summer's morning, was captivated by the sound of a faerie melody. He sat down beneath a tree to listen. When the last strains of the music died away he stood up and was surprised to see that the tree above him, previously green and lush, had withered and died. Returning home, he found the house looked strangely different, somehow older and covered in ivy. There was an old man standing in the doorway, a stranger, who greeted Shon and asked him what he wanted. Shon, surprised, replied that he had left his father and mother in that very house but minutes before. The old man asked his name. 'Shon ap Shenkin', replied the boy. The old man became deathly pale and replied, 'I often heard my grandfather, your father, speak of your disappearance'. At this Shon ap Shenkin crumbled to dust on the doorstep.

SPRIGGANS

Spriggans are dour and ugly and grotesque in shape. Although quite small, they have the ability to inflate themselves into monstrous forms which has led humans to believe them to be the ghosts of old giants.

Apart from their useful function as guardians of hill treasure, Spriggans are an infamous band of villains, skilled thieves, thoroughly destructive and often dangerous. They are quite capable of robbing human houses, kidnapping children (and leaving a repulsive baby Spriggan in exchange), causing whirlwinds to destroy fields of corn, blighting crops and all manner of other unpleasant mischief.

There is a story, told by Robert Hunt in his *'Popular Romances of the West of England'* (1865), of an old woman in whose cottage a band of Spriggan thieves used to meet nightly to divide up their booty. The Spriggans invariably left a coin for the old woman but she was determined to have more. One night she turned her shift inside out, turning clothes being as effective as iron or Holy Water in repulsing faeries. In this way she gained all the Spriggans' loot, although they avenged themselves to some extent as the old woman subsequently suffered agonies every time she wore the shift.

THE MISER ON THE FAERIE GUMP

A certain hill in Cornwall named the Gump, near St. Just, is a reputed meeting place for the faeries who have often been seen there, gaily attired and making merry with music, feasting and dancing. Despite the faeries' usual dislike of intruders, well-mannered onlookers were welcomed and occasionally even given small but precious gifts.

There was an old miser, however, who planned to reap benefit from the faerie gathering. One night he set out to steal all he could from the little people. He started to climb the hill and soon heard music under his feet although he could see nothing. As he climbed higher the music grew louder and suddenly the hill opened in front of his eyes. A stream of little people poured out, a bevy of musicians, a troop of soldiers and a hideous band of Spriggans, the guardians of Cornish faerie hills and treasure. At the sight of this evil-looking bodyguard the miser hesitated for an instant but was undaunted as he was far bigger than any of the faeries.

The hill itself meanwhile was lit up by thousands of jewels twinkling from every blade of grass and the miser gazed in wonderment at the tables being set with finest gem-encrusted gold and silverware. Then the faerie court appeared in all its finery and the faerie prince and princess moved to the high table, the most magnificently bedecked of all. The miser resolved that this would be his object and prepared to swoop on the riches laid out there. Too late he noticed the Spriggans had cast shining ropes around him and he saw that every eye was on him. Suddenly all was plunged into darkness. He was jerked sharply sideways onto his back, pierced all over and pinched from head to foot. With the dawn the miser found himself flat on his back at the foot of the mound, covered with dewy cobwebs . . .

A tale is told of an encounter between faeries and smugglers where the Spriggans played a far more terrifying role. A small band of smugglers came ashore one night near Long Rock in Cornwall. Having heaved all their booty out of their boat and up over the high-water mark on the shore, three of the men departed to see to the necessary arrangements for the sale of their goods whilst three others, including Tom Warren of Paul, reputed as one of the boldest smugglers of his day, lay down to rest. Hardly had they dozed off when they were aroused by a shrill whistling sound and a tinkling. Believing this to be the sound of young people making merry, Tom went to warn them to be off. He climbed a high sand-bank and saw, a short distance away, in hollows between other banks of sand, a company of gaily attired people of doll-like size skipping and dancing about, spotlighted by flickering lights. On a high bank amidst the revellers he saw a group of little, old and bearded men blowing mouth-organs, beating cymbals and tambourines, playing jew's harps and tweeting on whistles made of reeds.

The little men were all dressed in green with scarlet caps and as they played their beards waggled about. Tom was highly amused at this sight and just could not resist shouting out 'Will e be shaved – will e be shaved old red-caps?'. He hailed them twice in this manner and was on the point of doing so again when all the dancers, and hundreds more than he had at first noticed, sprang up into ranks, armed with bows and arrows, spears and slings. To the accompaniment of a military march, the Spriggans stamped towards Tom, getting bigger and bigger as they approached. Their fearsome aspect so appalled Tom that he fled back to his comrades, roused them and urged them to put to sea for their lives. As they ran towards the boat, a hail of small stones rained on them and 'burned like coals o' fire wherever they hit them'. The men were so frightened that they pulled far out to sea before they dared look back although they knew they were safe as no Spriggan dares touch salt water. When they did cast a glance behind them they saw an army of the ugliest-looking creatures possible lined along the shore making threatening gestures. It was not until daybreak when horses were heard approaching that the little people retreated to the sandbanks.

FAERIES
ON THE
EASTERN
GREEN

FAERIE ISLANDS

One of the most persistent and recurring themes in European mythology is that of the Isles of the Blest, or Fortunate Isles, lying in the western sea, beyond the setting sun. The Irish seem to have more islands, or more names for the same islands, than anybody else. Some of the best known perhaps are Tir Nan Og, the Land of the Young; Tirfo Thuinn, the Land Under the Waves; Tire Nam Beo, Land of the Living; Tirn Aill, the Other World; Mag Mor, the Great Plain; Mag Mell, the Pleasant Plain; Tir Tairngire, the Plain of Happiness.

These islands, whether the homes of faeries, Gods or the dead, are, as their names suggest, lands where all is happiness, peace and plenty. There are no frosts or droughts for it is always Spring. There is no ageing or disease or work, for all things grow in abundance without need of ploughing or sowing and there is always fruit on the trees.

It was to Tir Nan Og that the Tuatha de Danann fled before the advancing Milesians and that land gives them all that they could wish for . . . They spend their days feasting, hunting, love-making and enjoying beautiful music. They can even indulge their passion for battles, as those killed one day can arise with their wounds healed the next.

Some of these islands float and some are submerged, raising themselves above the surface only at night or, in the case of Hy-Breasail as recorded by Giraldus Cambrensis, once in seven years. These islands can be made to remain on the surface only if fire or steel is brought upon them and Hy-Breasail remained there after a red-hot arrow was fired into it. It still eludes those who search for it, however, even though it has been marked on early maps and several major expeditions have been mounted by the merchants of Bristol, amongst others, to find it . It is usually depicted as round, divided in two by a wide river which is not unlike Plato's description of Atlantis.

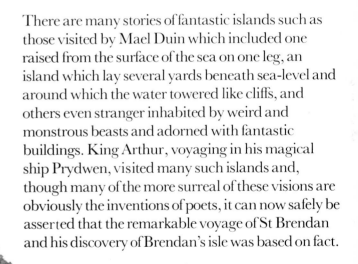

There are many stories of fantastic islands such as those visited by Mael Duin which included one raised from the surface of the sea on one leg, an island which lay several yards beneath sea-level and around which the water towered like cliffs, and others even stranger inhabited by weird and monstrous beasts and adorned with fantastic buildings. King Arthur, voyaging in his magical ship Prydwen, visited many such islands and, though many of the more surreal of these visions are obviously the inventions of poets, it can now safely be asserted that the remarkable voyage of St Brendan and his discovery of Brendan's isle was based on fact.

Sailors passing near Gresholm Island, off the coast of
Wales have glimpsed the 'Green Meadows of
Enchantment', a land just visible beneath the
surface of the sea.

It was Manannan, son of Lêr who, as chief deity of the sea, held sway over many of these islands and it was he who summoned Bran, son of Febal, to Emhain, the Island of Women. This was believed to be a vast country supported in the sea on four huge bronze pillars and inhabited solely by beautiful women. The journey took them past the Island of Delight, the inhabitants of which behaved as though intoxicated, gesticulating and shouting with laughter. When one of Bran's men landed on the island, he started acting in the same manner so Bran was forced to continue without him. When they reached Emhain, they found it more than matched their expectations and they were entertained royally. After a year had passed, however, they began to long to see Ireland again and, promising to obey the women's strictures not to set foot on dry land, they set sail. When they approached the shores of Ireland, Bran called to some of the inhabitants and told them his name. They answered that the only Bran, son of Febal known to them was the one whose voyage to seek the land of women was the subject of some of their oldest legends. On hearing this one of Bran's companions waded ashore but, on touching dry land, he immediately crumbled to dust. Bran stayed awhile near the shore to relate his adventures and then turned his boats about and sailed away, never to be seen again.

There is a VIIth-century Irish poem relating how Manannan mac Lir, driving his chariot across the tops of the waves, watches with amusement and sings as Bran journeys in his coracle through what to him is the sea, but to Manannan is the sky above a fertile plain . . .

'Bran deems it a marvellous beauty
In his coracle across the clear sea:
While to me in my chariot from afar
It is a flowery plain on which he rides about.

'What is a clear sea
For the prowed skiff in which Bran is,
That is a happy plain with profusion of flowers
To me from the chariot of two wheels.

'Along the top of a wood has swum
Thy coracle across ridges,
There is a wood of beautiful fruit
Under the prow of thy little skiff.

'A wood with blossom and fruit,
On which is the vine's veritable fragrance;
A wood without decay, without defect,
On which are leaves of a golden hue.'

OISIN

One of the few mortal men to be invited to Tir Nan Og was Oisin (Isheen), son of Finn, chief of the legendary Fenian warriors of Ireland. The Fenians were out hunting one day when a lady of great beauty approached them. She was Niamh of the Golden Hair, daughter of Manannan and she chose Oisin from amongst them to be her lover. She bade him mount up behind her on her faerie steed and they rode over the land to the sea and then across the tops of the waves towards the enchanted land of Tir Nan Og 'the most delightful country to be found of greatest repute under the sun'. They saw wondrous sights as they journeyed. Faerie palaces appeared on the surface of the sea. At one of these Niamh asked Oisin to set free a Tuatha de Danan damsel who was a prisoner of a Fomor, one of the demons of the deep sea. Oisin fought the Fomor and set the girl free.

Soon they reached the Land of the Young and Oisin remained there with his love for three hundred years before he remembered his home and the Fenians and had a sudden yearning to see them again. He asked leave to visit his homeland. Niamh furnished him with a faerie steed for the journey but warned Oisin at all costs not to let his feet touch earthly soil. Oisin gave his word to take care and swiftly reached Ireland. However he found all had changed from the land he remembered. Finn and the Fenians had become a legend of the past. The Battle of Gabhra had been fought and St Patrick had converted the land. Even the men seemed different, smaller, almost dwarflike compared to the men he remembered. Oisin noticed three of them trying vainly to lift a great stone. He stooped to lift it for them with one hand but as he did so his golden saddle-girth snapped and he fell to the ground. Immediately the faerie horse vanished and Oisin was transformed into an ancient blind old man.

A number of ballads recount how St Patrick found Oisin stranded on earthly soil in his hopeless old age and took him into his house. The saint did his best to convert Oisin to Christianity, describing the wonders of the Heaven that could be his if only he would repent. But Oisin replied that he could not conceive of a Heaven that would not be proud to receive the Fenians if they wished to enter it or a God who would not be honored to count Finn amongst his friends. If however this was the case, what was the point of an eternal life with no hunting or wooing of beautiful women? He would prefer to go to the Hell where, according to St Patrick, his Fenian comrades lay in anguish, and die as he had lived.

O'DONOGHUE

Lough Lean in Ireland, now called the lake of Killarney, is the home of O'Donoghue, once the ruler of the surrounding land. He walked out one day upon the surface of the lake, watched by all the members of his court, and slowly sank into the depths to claim his new kingdom.

Every May Day morning he leaves the magnificent palace which is said to lie at the bottom of the lake and visits his old domain.

It has been some years since O'Donoghue last made his appearance. On that day T. Crofton Croker tells us in his *Fairy Legends and Traditions of the South of Ireland*, 'the first beams of the rising sun were just gilding the lofty summit of Glenaa, when the waters near the eastern shore of the lake became suddenly and violently agitated, though all the rest of its surface lay smooth and still as a tomb of polished marble. The next moment a foaming wave darted forward, and, like a proud high-crested warhorse, exulting in his strength, rushed across the lake toward Toomies mountian. Behind this wave appeared a stately warrior fully armed, mounted upon a milk-white steed; his snowy plume waved gracefully from a helmet of polished steel, and at his back fluttered a light blue scarf. The horse, apparently exulting in his noble burden, sprung after the wave along the water, which bore him up like firm earth, while showers of spray that glittered brightly in the morning sun were dashed up at every bound.'

The warrior was O'Donoghue and in his wake followed a bevy of young people who glided over the water, linked together with garlands of spring flowers, to the time of sweet unearthly music. Having almost reached the western side of the lake, O'Donoghue turned his steed towards the wood-fringed shore of Glenaa followed by his train of attendants. They then slowly disappeared into the mists floating over the lake and the magical strains of their music gradually died away 'and the hearers awoke as from a dream of bliss'.

Many Faeries
have their
homes in
lakes.
In the case
of The Lady
of the Lake,
the surface
of the
water was
an illusion
created by
magic
to disguise
her palace.

There is a legend of a submerged town in one of the many lakes in Wales said to be the home of Gwragedd Annwn (Gwrageth anoon). Some people have seen towers and battlements beneath the surface of the water and heard the peal of bells.

THE GWRAGEDD ANNWN

The Gwragedd Annwn (Gwrageth anoon) are
Welsh water faeries, beautiful Lake Maidens who
occasionally take mortals to be their husbands.
One well-known legend tells of a young man
who used to graze his cattle by a small lake
near the Black Mountains. One day he saw a most
enchanting creature rowing gently to and fro in a
golden boat on the surface of the lake.
He fell deeply in love with her and offered her
some of the bread he had brought from home for his
midday meal. She answered that the bread was too
hard and disappeared into the depths. The young
man's mother gave him some unbaked dough to
take with him the next day and he offered this
to the faerie but she answered that it was too soft
and again disappeared. On the third day his mother
gave him some lightly baked bread and this passed
muster. Three figures rose from the lake, an old man
with a beautiful daughter on either side of him. The
girls were identical and the father told the young
farmer that he was willing to offer him the daughter
with whom he was in love if he could point
her out. The farmer would have given up in despair
but one slightly moved her foot and he,
recognising her slipper, won her hand.

The water-faerie was given a fine dowry and they
lived together happily. However, the young farmer
had been warned that he would lose his beautiful wife
should he strike her three times causelessly. It so
happened that, although they were indeed blissfully
happy, the Gwragedd Annwn had some curious
faerie ways; she might weep at a wedding or laugh
and sing at the funeral of a child and this eventually
led to her loving husband reproving her three times,
more by a love-tap than a blow, but this was enough
and she was forced to leave him. She did not forget
her sons however and taught them many secrets of
medicine so that they became famed physicians.

THE GWRAGEDD ANNWN

In other days, every New Year's morning a door was to be found open in a rock by a Welsh lake and those who dared enter came upon a secret passage which led them to a small island in the middle of the lake. Here they found themselves in an exquisite garden inhabited by the Gwragedd Annwn who feted their guests, pressing on them all manner of fruit and flowers and entertaining them with beautiful music. The faeries told their visitors many wondrous secrets and invited them to stay as long as they wished. However, they warned them that the island was a secret and nothing from it should be taken away.

One day it so happened that a visitor to the magic garden pocketed a flower he had been offered, thinking it would bring him luck. The moment the thief touched 'unhallowed' land again however, the flower vanished and he fell unconscious. Other guests to the enchanted land were bid farewell with customary politeness but since that day the door to the beautiful garden has remained firmly closed.

TUATHA DE DANANN

Following their defeat by the Milesians, those of the Tuatha de Danann who decided to stay in Ireland made their homes under the hollow hills or 'Raths' where they became the Daoine Sidhe. The Tuatha de Danann were originally gigantic but, in the course of time and with the encroachment of Christianity, as they diminished in importance, they correspondingly dwindled in size.

The most important member of the Daoine Sidhe today is Finvarra, the High King of the Irish faeries who is also thought by some to be the King of the Dead. He still holds court in his palace beneath the faerie hill of Knockma.

The DAOINE SIDHE take great pleasure in fighting and are skilled chess-players. Many mortals have lost everything they possessed by daring to challenge Finvarra.

Womanizing is another of Finvarra's favorite
activities. Even though Oonagh, his wife, is the
most beautiful woman in our world or his,
he frequently abducts mortal women. One such
was Ethna the Bride who was eventually won
back by her persistent husband. He threatened
to dig down into Finvarra's Rath and expose the
interior to the light of day.

HURLING is as popular amongst
the Daoine Sidhe as it is with the Irish themselves.
There is an old story of a hurling match between
the faeries of Munster and those of Connaught in
which two humans were invited to take part.
(For some reason unknown to us it is considered
necessary for the faene host to include a living
man when fighting or hurling.)

In this tale the match turns into a fight in which the Connaught side quickly gained the upper hand. The host of Munster then transformed themselves into flying beetles and ate every green thing in sight, destroying the countryside as they went until, suddenly thousands of doves rose from a hole in the ground and devoured the marauding beetles.

Faerie ways

The faerie temperament is a complex one and the behavior of the little people is governed by a code of ethics far removed from our own. Most faeries, whatever their size, appearance or character, have powers of some kind and can bestow good or ill luck at will so the more we know about them, the more likely we are to emerge from an encounter unscathed. Careful handling and respect in faerie dealings are of paramount importance. Only too easily is offence taken and woe betide he who is tempted to take liberties . . .

The faerie tendency to be mischievous and sometimes spiteful (and in some cases positively dangerous) has resulted in the use of placatory terms when referring to them – names like 'Good Neighbours', 'Mother's Blessing', the 'Good People', 'Wee Folk' (implying harmlessness). General behavior patterns amongst the faeries vary considerably but some are indisputably inherently bad and no amount of correct behaviour, kindness or wooing could conceivably mellow them. Indeed it is positively dangerous to approach these creatures. Certain female faeries are particularly malevolent, made more deadly perhaps by their beautiful appearance which entices unwary men to an untimely and horrible doom.

While the realm of Faerie is, to a great extent, dependent on the world of mortals and many faerie beings, such as the Brownies, actually attach themselves to human households (Banshees and Buttery Spirits could also be described as being 'attached' to human households but their motives are very different . . .), the path towards a faerie amity is fraught with danger and should be trodden with extreme caution. Many are the helpful Brownies who have reverted to the role of churlish and troublesome Boggarts when offended or even teased and terrible is the revenge of the faerie angered.

From time immemorial man has maintained an ambivalent relationship with the world of Faerie, for while faerie contact can unquestionably be beneficial, it is just as likely to be baneful.

In other days any unaccountable deaths of animals and humans were believed to be due to 'Elf-shot'. Small flint arrowheads, which we now know were made by Stone-Age man, were attributed to the elves. Where no physical shot was in evidence it was assumed the arrowhead made no wound but instead induced paralysis. The victim could then be carried away to Faerie while a replica body was left behind to sicken and die. 'Stroke', in the sense of paralytic seizure, is a word we still use, probably unaware that it originally meant 'Elf-stroke'.

Other human malaises, such as rheumatism, cramps and bruising, were also exclusively ascribed to Faerie – caused by pinching faerie fingers, a penalty for incurring faerie displeasure. Marston, in *Mountebanke's Masque* says:

> If lustie Doll, maide of the Dairie,
> Chance to be blew nipt by the Fairie . . .

which strikes one immediately as rather a convenient theory.

Additionally, consumption, a wasting disease, was blamed on compulsive visits at night to the faerie hills, leaving the victims weak and exhausted in the morning. Infantile paralysis was of course due to the baby in reality being a changeling – in fact, any deformities such as lame legs and hunched backs were induced by the elves, according to the lore of the day. Shakespeare would seem to have endorsed this belief:

> Thou Elvish-marked, abortive, rooting hog.
> *Richard III*

Other well-known faerie annoyances include the disappearance of small objects. There is even one kind of faerie, called 'Alp-Luachra' by the Irish but dubbed a 'Joint-eater' or 'Just-halver' by Robert Kirk in his book *The Secret Commonwealth* (1691) who sits invisibly beside his victim and shares his food with him 'feeding on the Pith or Quintessence of what the Man eats; and that therefoir he continues Lean like a Hawke or Heron, notwithstanding his devouring Appetite;'

Although we now have a clearer understanding of some of the causes (other than elves) of many human ills, the close connection between Faerie and the plant world undoubtedly accounts for the blights and diseases which sometimes destroy entire crops. These devastations are very probably a punishment for human transgression of some kind.

Of course it is usually the small irritations in life that are actually caused by the mischievous faerie. Tangles in human hair and horses' manes are better known as elf-locks. Queen Mab for one . . .

> 'plats the manes of horses in the night;
> And bakes the elf-locks in foulsluttish hairs,
> Which once untangled much misfortune
> bodes.'

PROTECTION AGAINST FAERIES

Wary country folk have discovered numerous
methods of discouraging the more troublesome faerie
attentions. Those walking alone at night are
particularly vulnerable and there are various proven
methods of self-protection for the different risks.
Effective devices and objects include the following:

Turning clothes inside out
(a glove turned inside out and
tossed into a faerie ring will disperse
the revellers)

Bells

Iron - eg. a knife in a doorway,
a nail in the pocket,
open scissors hung above a baby's cot.

The Bible
Running Water
Bread
A Crucifix or Cross (Also, when marked
on the top of cakes,
this dissuades the faeries
from dancing on them)

Salt

Holy Prayers

Rowan and Red Thread
(In the case of the Scots, a
red ribbon attached over the
front door or tied to the tails
of cattle — this was to discourage
witches. Elsewhere a red
cloth was sometimes tied round
children's chests as protection
against the little people)

Ancient churchyard mold
Daisy chains
Stones with holes (to protect horses)
Horseshoes (moon symbol and iron combined)
Flax on the floor
Shoes placed with toes pointing away from the bed
A sock under the bed
A knife under the pillow
A twig of Broom
A pig's head or pentsgram drawn on the door
The burning of thorns on top of a faerie hill will release captive children.
St John's Wort.

An Anglo-Saxon leechcraft anti-elf cocktail: Rub myrrh into wine, and an equal quantity of white incense. Shave a little off an agate stone and add to wine. Drink this after a night's fasting, or three mornings, or nine or twelve.

Old time May Day fertility rites always utilized the sun symbol daisy to protect the participants from the faeriefolk who are particularly active at such significant times of the year. Among other protective devices were the bells on the legs of the dancing Morris Men – these bells are still, happily, in use today.

While at times the faeries are perfectly capable of being morose, vitriolic or even savagely revengeful, they are also indisputably the world's greatest practical jokers and their penchant for pranks is shared by even the best of the good faeries. This basically good-humored mischief is very evident where such beings as the Hedley Kow are concerned:

The Hedley Kow was a bogie, mischievous rather than malignant, which haunted the village of Hedley, near Ebchester. His appearance was never very alarming, and he used to end his frolics with a horse laugh at the expense of his victims. He would present himself to some old dame gathering sticks, in the form of a truss of straw, which she would be sure to take up and carry away. Then it would become so heavy she would have to lay her burden down, on which the straw would become 'quick', rise upright, and shuffle away before her, till at last it vanished from her sight with a laugh and shout.

William Henderson in his *Notes on the Folk-Lore of the Northern Counties of England and the Borders* (1879) also tells us how the Kow loved to disrupt life in the farmhouse 'for it is said to have constantly imitated the voice of the servant-girl's lovers, overturned the kailpot, given the cream to the cats, unravelled the knitting, or put the spinning-wheel out of order.' Other favorite tricks of the mischievous faeries include misleading unwary travellers (this is sometimes called *pixy-leading*) and scaring people.

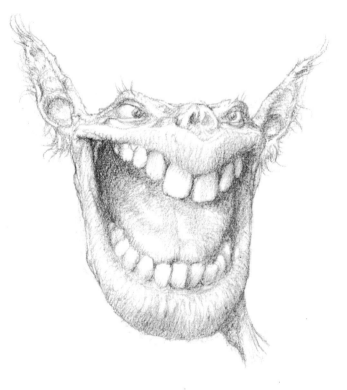

The faerie attitude towards humans meanwhile has a curiously moralistic bias. They expect a particular mode of behaviour to be adhered to in their regard, set high standards of orderliness for human homes they habitually visit yet forbid any prying eyes when they do. Faeries like cheerful, generous humans and are particularly sympathetic towards lovers. They like food and wine to be left for them at night, yet they are very temperate.

The Irish Sidhe (Shee) faeries passionately love beauty and luxury and have a total contempt for thrift and economy. Lady Wilde in her *Ancient Legends of Ireland* remarks how they detest 'the close, niggard hand that gathers the last grain, and drains the last drop in the milk-pail, and plucks the tree bare of fruit, leaving nothing for the spirits who wander by in the moonlight'.

The lazy or dishonest will be punished with pinching, cramps or even lameness and worse. The kitchen maid who omits to sweep out the hearth and set out clean water for the faerie babies to bathe in does so at her risk while her conscientious attention to these details could well bring her a gift of money in her shoe when she wakes and much good luck . . .

Reliability and kindness are usually repaid with good luck, gifts or practical help and faeries can be extravagant. There is the tale told of the unfortunate Bill Doody, sitting by the Lake of Killarney and pondering over the insoluble problem of rent-day . . . 'That lake', W. B. Yeats tells us 'glittering in sunshine, sprinkled with fairy isles of rock and verdure, and bounded by giant hills of ever-varying hues, might, with its magic beauty, charm all sadness but despair. . .'. However from it came salvation for Bill Doody. A tall gentleman appeared who, on hearing of Bill's plight, poured 'a purse full of gold into Bill's old hat, which in his grief he had flung on the ground' and disappeared before Bill could thank him.

On the morrow Bill Doody proceeded to his hard-hearted agent to pay his rent, proudly paid what was owed and left, having taken care to procure a receipt for his gold. 'The agent going to his desk shortly after, was confounded at beholding a heap of gingerbread cakes instead of the money he had deposited there. He raved and swore, but all to no purpose; the gold had become gingerbread cakes, just marked like the guineas, with the king's head; and Bill had the receipt in his pocket.' Yeats goes on to say that 'from that hour Bill Doody grew rich; all his undertakings prospered; and he often blesses the day that he met with O'Donoghue, the great prince that lives down under the lake of Killarney.'

Nevertheless, he who receives faerie graces must not talk of them for faerie etiquette demands secrecy. Strangely, the behaviour required for the maintenance of friendly relations with the 'good neighbors' excludes not only disclosure of faerie help or gifts to other mortals but also expression of thanks. Should a grateful human misguidedly attempt to thank a hardworking but ragged Pixie or Brownie with a gift of fine clothing, no thanks will be forthcoming – the little helper will almost always take umbrage and depart, never to be seen again.

Another strange quirk of faerie nature concerns loans. Should a mortal borrow faerie utensils or food, he would cause great offence if, in gratitude, he proffered more than he originally borrowed. The faeries, however, return loans of grain with generous interest although they always give back barley for oats.

It frequently occurs that faerie gifts and rewards are merely the products of illusion and soon revert to their original forms.

Faeries have a rather curious code of ethics for themselves. Whilst there is a definite code of honor between the different denizens of the faerie world (and a tale is told of the poor unfortunate trow boy banished for ever from Trowland for stealing a silver spoon from another Trow), a faerie will have no qualms at appropriating victuals, goods and livestock from mortals. Sometimes, as in the case of the Brownie who sat between two greedy servant girls and consumed most of the stolen junket they were eating, faeries will take advantage of their magic powers to remove food from under the very noses of those about to eat it.

Disturbingly, this faerie pilfering does not stop short of mortals, and particularly human babies who are greatly valued to inject new blood into this dwindling race. Golden-haired babes are at greatest risk and mortal mothers should take all possible precautions to guard their offspring until they are safely baptised. Again, mortal midwives are often spirited away into the land of faerie to care for a faerie baby.

Dependence on humans among certain types of faeries is very significant. For example, every seven years, the land of Faerie has to pay a tithe of *TEIND* to Hell and human captives are used as payment. The most common way of taking a human is to steal a human baby and leave a faerie changeling in its place. This changeling can be an ugly old elf or even a manufactured one of wood but, under a faerie enchantment, it appears to be an exact replica of the stolen child. Sometimes it then seems to die and so is buried, while the real baby is brought up in Faerieland to inject a dwindling and weak stock with a fresh, healthy human strain. It might eventually be offered as part of the septannual tithe.

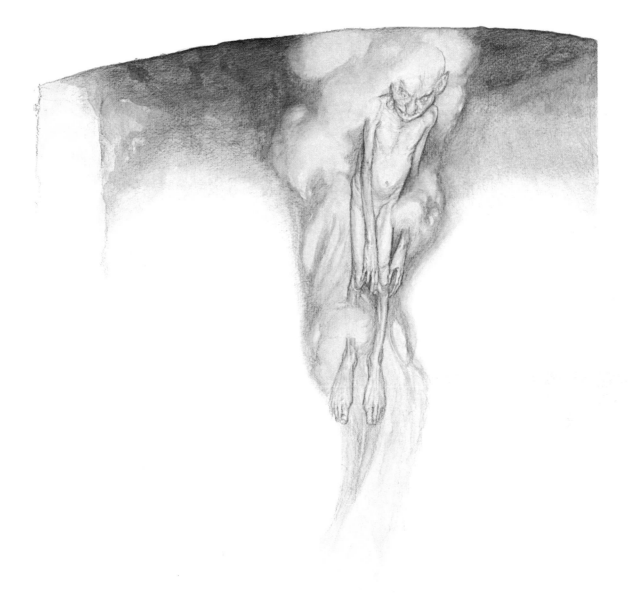

Should the baby replica not die, it may develop a wizened or deformed appearance, or be sickly and fretful, or else have a voracious appetite. The changeling can be forced to betray its faerie nature by various means. One is to place it on a red-hot shovel or throw it on the fire. It will then fly up the chimney. A less brutal and more common method is to go through the motions of brewing water in empty halves of eggshells. The changeling, noticing this, sits up and in a strange old voice declares, 'I have seen the egg before the hen. I have seen the first acorn before the oak. But I have never seen brewing in an eggshell before', thus revealing its ancient age. It can then be thrown on the fire from which, laughing and shrieking, it will fly up the chimney. The true baby will then very likely be found at the door.

It has occasionally occurred that a little person has been captured by humans. Sadly these are always the most vulnerable and harmless of their race and they almost always pine and die in captivity when escape is impossible. Perhaps the most famous example of this is Ralph of Coggeshall's account of The Green Children of which Thomas Keightley has given an English translation in his book *Fairy Mythology*: The events took place in Suffolk:

A boy and his sister were found by the inhabitants of that place near the mouth of a pit which is there, who had the form of all their limbs like to those of other men, but they differed in the colour of their skin from all the people of our habitable world; for the whole surface of their skin was tinged of a green colour. No one could understand their speech. When they were brought as curiosities to the house of a certain knight, Sir Richard de Calne, at Wikes, they wept bitterly. Bread and other victuals were set before them, but they would touch none of them, although they were tormented by great hunger, as the girl afterwards acknowledged. At length, when some beans just cut, with their stalks, were brought into the house, they made signs, with great avidity, that they should be given to them. When they were brought, they opened the stalks instead of the pods, thinking the beans were in the hollow of them, but not finding them there, they began to weep anew.

When those who were present saw this, they opened the pods, and showed them the naked beans. They fed on these with great delight, and for a long time tasted no other food. The boy, however, was always languid and depressed, and he died within a short time. The girl enjoyed continual good health; and becoming accustomed to various kinds of food, lost completely that green colour, and gradually recovered the sanguine habit of her entire body. She was afterwards regenerated by the laver of holy baptism, and lived for many years in the service of that knight (as I have frequently heard from him and his family), and was rather loose and wanton in her conduct. Being frequently asked about the people of her country, she asserted that the inhabitants and all they had in that country, were of a green colour; and that they saw no sun, but enjoyed a degree of light like what is after sunset. Being asked how she came into this country with the aforesaid boy, she replied, that as they were following their flocks, they came to a certain cavern, on entering which they heard a delightful sound of bells; ravished by whose sweetness, they went for a long time wandering on through the cavern, until they came to its mouth. When they came out of it, they were struck senseless by the excessive light of the sun, and they thus lay for a long time. Being terrified by the noise of those who came on them, they wished to fly, but they could not find the entrance of the cavern before they were caught.

Faeries have the ability to render themselves visible or invisible to the mortal eye at will and they can be simultaneously visible to one person whilst invisible to another. However they can at times be espied without their knowledge. This is normally while they are at work or engaged in faerie revels when they are discovered by humans who come across them unawares or by those determined enough to use devious methods to seek them out.

Time is often an essential ingredient as most faerie sightings take place either at noon, when the sun is at its zenith, or alternatively at midnight and in the twilight hours preceding sunset and sunrise, all of which mark the transition from light to dark or vice versa. It should also be noted that dawn can also be the moment of escape for humans on whom faerie spells have been cast.

May Day (which celebrates the return to the summer solstice), Midsummer's Eve and Halloween (which to the Celts marked the changeover from the old celtic year to the new) are especially favorable times for a sighting. This transition element is also important where people are concerned and it explains why growing children and, particularly, young girls just prior to puberty are far more likely than adults to see the little people. It is for this reason in fact that a wise parent will take care on May Day to ensure his children wear clothing adorned with bells or carry daisy chains as these will ward off danger from faeries.

In general terms, faeries do not like to be seen by humans so the gaze of the observer must be steady for the little people will disappear in the blink of an eye.

There is also a square yard of turf somewhere in Wales which gives a single glimpse of Faerie to anyone who stumbles across it. However, it keeps its secret well for the exact spot can never be found twice.

The naked eye, which is generally unable to see the faerie in its invisible state, can be 'opened' when a mortal carries a four-leaved clover. A story is told of a milkmaid who happened by chance to have picked a four-leaved clover with the grass she used to soften the weight of the pail on her head. When she next looked at the cow she saw dozens of faeries taking turns to milk her.

The application of faerie ointment to the eyelids (this ointment is normally reserved for anointing the eyes of faerie babies with mortal mothers), also dispels the illusions cast by faeries to conceal their true appearance. However, the mortal who dares enhance his vision with the forbidden ointment risks incurring faerie wrath. There are those who have been blinded in punishment. A tale is told of a young girl who takes up service as a nursemaid to the small son of a widower. He is, unbeknown to her, one of the little people. She applies the ointment to her own eyes out of curiousity, betrays her vision of the faerie world yet is allowed to leave unharmed. However, this is certainly the exception rather than the rule.

In the story of Eilian of Garth Dorwen, Eilian the servant maid escaped with the Tylwyth Teg (Terlooeth teig) faeries of Wales and was seen no more until one night her old mistress, who was also a midwife, was summoned to help a birth. The woman was taken to a large cave within which there was a magnificent room where the wife lay on a fine bed. After the birth of the baby, the husband asked the midwife to anoint the baby's eyes. Having done so, the midwife rubbed one of her own eyes that was itching and with that eye suddenly saw herself to be in a poor cave with large stones all about and a little fire in one corner. The wife, lying on a bundle of rushes and withered ferns, was none other than Eilian, her former servant girl.

Not long afterwards the old midwife went to market where she saw the husband and enquired after Eilian's health. He replied that his wife was well but asked with which eye the midwife saw him. On hearing which eye it was, he put it out with a bulrush.

Faeries are usually well camouflaged

The protective camouflage used by the faeries is
generally termed 'glamour' and is often designed to
deceive mortals into believing they are dealing with
their own kind. Glamour...

> Could make a ladye seem a knight,
> A nutshell seem a gilded barge
> A sheeling seem a palace large
> And youth seem age and age seem youth
> All was delusion, nought was truth.
> *The Lay of the Last Minstrel*
> REGINALD SCOT

Robert Kirk in his book *Secret Commonwealth, and Essay of the Nature and Actions of the Subterranean (and, for the most Part) Invisible People, heretofioir going under the name of Elves, Faunes and Fairies, or the lyke, among the Low-Country Scots as they are described by those who have the Second Sight . . .* (1691) pinned down the elusiveness of faerie essence. They are 'of a middle nature betwixt man and angel', and have 'light changeable Bodies (lyke those called Astral); somewhat of the nature of a condensed cloud, and best seen in twilight. These Bodies be so plyable through the subtilty of the spirits that agitate them, that they can make them appear or disappear at pleasure'. This is only logical in view of the fact that faeries have the ability to control their own size, an art known as *shape-shifting*. At will they can become immense in stature or magically shrink to the size of the merest speck of dust. They can also drastically alter their appearance, assuming any guise they may desire. The importance of the faerie shape-changing ability cannot be over-emphasised. It affects every aspect of faerie life. Of course, some faeries also boast the power to transform the appearance or size of other faeries and also mortals – a warning to tread warily where the little people are concerned.

The faeries themselves come in an endless variety of shapes and sizes and a multitude of hues:
> Fairies, black, grey, green, and white
> You moonshine revellers, and shades of
>   night.

The Merry Wives of Windsor
WILLIAM SHAKESPEARE

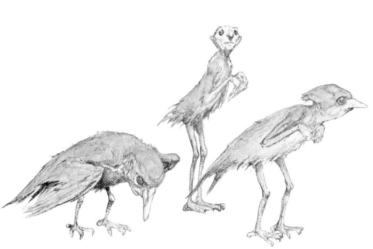

The Hyter Sprites of East Anglia have the ability to transform themselves into sand martins

One faerie, 'Yallery Brown', was discovered lying beneath a stone, cocooned in his long golden hair and beard

The life-cycle of the Cornish small people dictates that each shape-shifting operation leads to a minuscule reduction in normal size. This species diminishes in natural size gradually until the last stage in the cycle is reached and the faeries end their days as ants, or muryans as they are called in Cornwall.

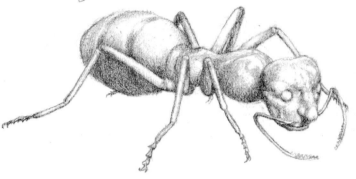

For this reason it is considered unlucky in Cornwall to kill ants.

We have no precise notion as to the average lifespan of a faerie. There have been some suggestions that they might be immortal yet there have been various sightings of faerie funerals which leads us to believe that they do eventually grow old and die as we do. However, there is absolutely no foundation for the quite widespread belief that every time a child voices disbelief in faeries, one of the little people drops down dead. Most authoritative documents on the life of faeries point to an existence of several hundreds of years.

William Blake, for one, reports having seen a procession of faeries, bearing a corpse on a rose leaf through his garden. At a certain spot, the deceased faerie was buried with due ceremony and chanting before the procession vanished. However, the suspicion remains that such 'burials,' like so many other faerie phenomena, are simply charades in which the little people mimic the behaviour of humans.

Sometimes they cannot be told apart from humans, at other times they resemble animals while they are often totally 'exceptional' in aspect. They can be enchantingly beautiful by human standards or, equally often, wizened, hairy and grotesquely ugly. However, how much of this external appearance is really *glamour* and how much reality is not for the mere human to know. Faerie beings also sometimes appear to radiate a shimmering light: 'Their fluid bodies half dissolved in light.' (Alexander Pope). Elsewhere tales are told of faeries whose presence is solely marked by a distinctly musty odour.

GHILLIE
DHU
A scottish
solitary faerie
who inhabits
certain birch
thickets.
His clothing
is made
of leaves
and moss.

It is very difficult to generalise on faerie appearance yet we know that, when they are not naked, faeries are most commonly observed wearing green coats or dresses with red caps, sometimes with the addition of a white owl's feather. The Tylwyth Teg of Wales have fair hair and wear white and the Silkies of the North of England are dressed in white silk. The more rustic solitary faeries sometimes wear clothing made from the most easily available materials such as moss and fallen leaves.

Giraldus Cambrensis wrote of XIIth-century Welsh faeries as follows:– 'These men were of the smallest stature, but very well-proportioned in their make; they were all of a fair complexion, with luxuriant hair falling over their shoulders like that of women. They had horses and greyhounds adapted to their size.'

Big or small, grotesque or dainty, most faerie types are characterized by a physical deformity of some kind which marks them out as 'different' to the trained observer. Such tell-tale signs include webbed or, more commonly still, back-to-front feet, or even goat's hoofs, noseless nostrils, long pendulous breasts and squint eyes. Pointed ears and cow's tails should also be taken as a warning that faeries are afoot.

Faeries spin, weave, build, churn and bake when not indulging in more pleasurable pastimes and their faerie powers enable them to accomplish prodigious feats with rather less than the effort this would demand from their human counterparts . . .

> When in one night, ere glimpse of morn
> His shadowy Flale hath thresh'd the Corn
> That ten day-labourers could not end.
> *L'Allegro*   JOHN MILTON

This power is also evident from the many stories in which a hideous dwarf tackles a seemingly impossible amount of spinning in order to win a human wife or obtain a human baby. The most famous example of this type of story is Rumpelstiltskin.

The little people are reputed to be fine gold and silversmiths and, typical of the complex faerie nature, are known, despite their fear of cold iron, to be excellent metalworkers. They possess cattle and dogs and most faerie animals have the peculiarity of being pure white with red eyes and ears.

The faeries savour the most natural foodstuffs. We know that they bake fine wholemeal breads and cakes (and they sometimes offer these as gifts to kind or helpful humans . . .), that they relish cow's milk straight from the udder (particularly from mortal cows and without permission . . .) and that they will gladly accept cheese and milksops as wages (if indeed they do not simply help themsleves). Lady Wilde reports in her *Ancient Legends of Ireland* (1899) that the little people 'love milk and honey, and sip the nectar from the cups of the flowers which is their fairy wine'. Giraldus Cambrensis meanwhile notes that the Welsh faeries 'ate neither flesh nor fish, but lived on a milk diet, made up into messes with saffron'.

However, in food as in every other facet of faerie life, one must wonder just what is truth and what is 'glamour'. Who is to divine with authority whether that silver goblet of heavenly mead is not an acorn filled with brackish water; that those royal banquet tables groaning under the weight of rare delicacies are not solely poor platters of faded autumn leaves, those luscious plums toadstools.

One thing is certain though – faerie food, like a faerie kiss, has special powers where humans are concerned and though tantalising in appearance can, with few exceptions, lead to the unwary being imprisoned forever in the land of faerie.

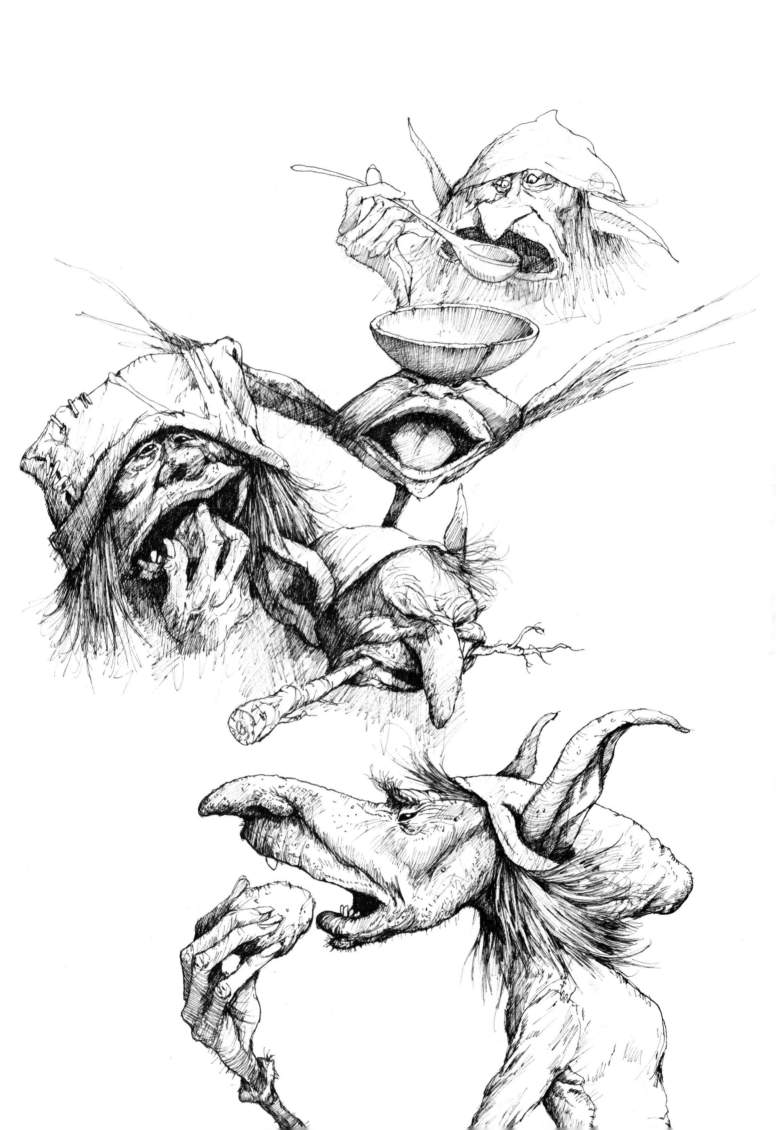

DENIZENS OF FAERIE

Man creates gods in his own image, and the gods which literature has handed down to us, Thor, Bran and Pallas Athene amongst others, reflect the aspirations, the love of war, honor and poetry of their worshippers who were basically the aristocrats of their respective societies.

However, the people who had no written language, and at whose dwellings the travelling Bards did not call, must have had their own divinities. They had local gods who looked after their crops, their houses and the vagaries of the weather. These deities could be blamed for tragedies and blessed for good fortune.

While the beliefs in Pantheons of thunder gods, war gods, gods of love and poetry has survived in classical and medieval manuscripts, the simpler rural gods have lived on by means of oral traditions as faeries.

The Irish have their own industrious faerie, the Leprechaun (lep-re-kawn) or one-shoe-maker. He is a solitary cobbler to be found merrily working on a single shoe (never a pair) beneath a dock leaf or under a hedge.

As with all faeries, it is important to see the Leprechaun before he sees you, for he then becomes more co-operative and can perhaps be persuaded to guide you to one of his hidden crocks of gold. But he is very sly and tricky and quite likely to disappear in the twinkling of an eye.

Gold is a rare prize.

There is an old Irish legend of a young boy who drove a turf cart to make a living. He was quiet and moody—it was even rumoured that he was a changeling—and what he loved most in the world was books. He read as much as his poor circumstances allowed. One day he read in an old book that Leprechauns knew all the secret places where gold weas hidden. With such gold he could buy all the books he desired. So, as the days passed, he watched and listened sharply for the click of a hammer in the hedgerow. At last one evening in the setting sun he saw a Leprechaun under a dock leaf. The boy crept up on him from behind, seized him by the scruff of his neck and refused to let go until hidden gold was revealed. 'There is no need for force', said the little fellow, 'for you and I are cousins once removed!' The boy had indeed been a changeling baby and since only those of faerie blood could possess the gold he was perfectly eligible. The gold lay in an old fort and they passed through a door in a stone wall. The ground was covered with gold pieces.

'Take what you want', said the Leprechaun, 'but quickly, for when the door shuts, it shuts for ever'. So the boy gathered as much as he could and took it outside. He was just returning for more when, with a tremendous crack, the door shut firm. The Leprechaun was nowhere to be seen. The gold was banked in Dublin. The boy was indeed rich; his money was spent wisely and he grew into a man of great learning and wisdom. His descendants are rich and prosperous to this day.

One detects a somewhat moralistic flavour to this tale—the good boy rewarded. Even though the subject was a changeling, Leprechauns are seldom so benign. They are characteristically tricky, merry and mischievous. For instance, in one case, a farmer was shown the only plant in a whole field of ragworts under which gold was buried. Not having a shovel with him he tied his red garter to the plant and went home to fetch the necessary tool. On his return every single ragwort sported a red garter.

LEPRECHAUNS
usually
wear
three cornered hats...

...... on occasions they have
been observed spinning like tops
using their headgear as an axis.

CLURICAUN

After his day's labors
the Leprechaun
enjoys a night's revelry
and then becomes known as
the Cluricaun (Kloor-a-kawn)
He raids wine cellars and is
known to take wild drunken
rides through the moonlight
on the backs of sheep
or shepherds' dogs.

The FIR DARRIG
(Fear dearg)
delights in practical
joking of a rather
gruesome nature and
therefore it is probably
safer to humor him...

GOBLINS

Goblins are a breed of small, swarthy, malicious beings – although 'goblin' as a term is often used as a general name for the uglier inhabitants of Faerie. They sometimes appear in the shape of animals which appropriately reflects their bestial nature. They are the thieves and villains of Faerie, companions to the dead, especially on Halloween:

> In that thrice hallow'd Eve abroad,
> When Ghosts, as Cottage-Maids believe,
> Their pebbled Beds permitted leave,
> And Goblins haunt from Fire or Fen,
> Or Mine, or Flood, the Walks of Men!

More than this, goblins are tempters, often using forbidden Faerie fruits to lure victims to their doom:

> We must not look at goblin men,
> We must not buy their fruits;
> Who knows upon what soil they fed,
> Their hungry thirsty roots?
>
> *Goblin Market*
> CHRISTINA GIORGINA ROSSETTI

Not all goblins are inherently evil. The mine dwelling goblins are generally benign towards man.

The Knockers who inhabit Cornish and Devon tin mines make the knocking noises that gave them their name to indicate rich veins of ore. They are generally friendly towards the miners although they enjoy making mischief. The Knocker is an exhibitionist and enjoys nothing more than teasing miners by pulling his already ugly face into even more horrible grimaces and performing grotesque dances.

A small piece of the miner's traditional underground meal, the pastie, should be left for the Knockers or they will be angry and bring ill luck. Whistling and swearing also annoy them and are rewarded with a shower of harmless faerie stones. Knockers are still active in the hundreds of abandoned Cornish tin mines waiting to lead an enterprising miner to a hidden wealthy lode.

However, the Knockers in an old mine at Chaw Gully, Dartmoor, are zealous guardians of their mine. Rich veins of tin and gold are said to be hidden in the mine's depths. High on a rocky point above the mine sit dark birds, silent and watching. If anyone should be intrepid enough to lower himself by rope into the black shaft, halfway down the birds croak, rasp a warning and a knife in a scrawny hand cuts the rope as well as the thread of life. Then the body is found neatly laid out at the top the following day.

KOBOLDS, the German version of the Knockers, are not so helpful, for they tend to be generally troublesome and mischievous, frustrating miners in their work and undoing labors. Nevertheless, sometimes they are unexpectedly helpful.

The WICHTLEIN from Southern Germany behave in much the same way. They announce the death of a miner by tapping three times. When a disaster is about to happen they are heard digging, pounding and imitating miners' work.

COBLYNAU

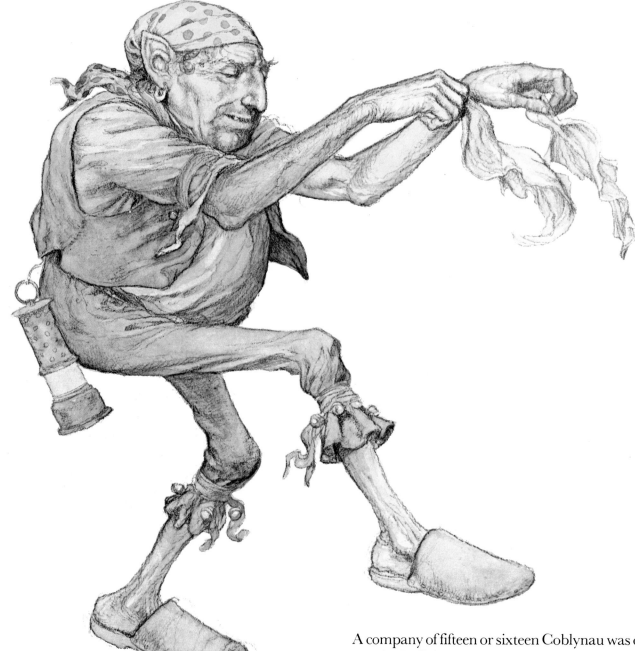

The Welsh have their own mine goblins called Coblynau (Koblernigh). They are the Welsh cousins to the Cornish Knockers. These creatures, using mining tools, are seen working industriously at the seam faces. The knocking of their picks and hammers is lucky, a sign of heavy ore content. However, for all their bustling labours, nothing is achieved for they are simply miming, thoroughly enjoying the imitation and pretence.

A company of fifteen or sixteen Coblynau was once seen in the Parish of Bodfari, Denbighshire, in the middle of a field dancing madly something after the manner of Morris-dancers, but with a wildness and swiftness in their motions'. The Coblynau were apparently dressed in red like British soldiers 'and wore red handkerchiefs spotted with yellow wound round their heads. And a strange circumstance about them was that although they were almost as big as ordinary men, yet they had unmistakably the appearance of dwarfs, and one could call them nothing but dwarfs'. (From *British Goblins* by Wirt Sikes).

DWARFS

Short but powerfully built, Dwarfs are generally bearded and aged in appearance, although this is because they reach maturity when only three years old and are grey-bearded by the age of seven. Their homes are the mountains of Scandinavia and Germany where they mine for precious metals to work into arms and armour and other artifacts which are often endowed with magic properties. It was the Dwarfs who fashioned Miolnir (the hammer of Thor), the spear Gungnir, the necklace Brisinga-men of Freya and innumerable other marvels, including a new head of hair for Thor's wife Sif and a rope strong enough to bind the giant wolf Fenris yet as slender as a thread.

Footnote: Dwarfs are extremely sensitive about showing their feet to anyone because they invariably have some deformity. They may, for example, be shaped like those of a goose, or a crow. Or they may point backwards. This is why dwarfs wear clothing that reaches to the ground. The curious can discover more by strewing ashes or flour in their path and studying the resulting footprints.

DWARFS cannot
appear above the
ground during the day.
One ray of sunlight would
turn them to stone.

According to some
accounts they spend
the daylight hours
as toads.

A DUERGAR* STORY

A story is told of a
traveler who, being lost in
bad weather saw a light
glimmering a short
distance away.
He found a rough
stone hut lit by
a dying fire   on either side
of the fire were two stones and
nearby two logs. He sat on
one and revived the fire with
some kindling and, shortly afterwards,
a Duergar entered and seated himself
opposite the traveler. There they sat
until the fire burnt down again. The
Duergar picked up one huge log and
broke it across his knees and placed it on
the fire. When it had burnt down
the Duergar indicated that the traveler
should put the other log on but the
traveler, suspecting a trick, did nothing.
So they sat until dawn when at once
the Duergar, the hut, and the fire disappeared
and the traveler found himself sitting
on the edge of a tall crag. If he
had moved to get the log
he would have fallen to his death.

* a malicious species
of dwarf from the
North of England

BROWN MAN
OF THE MUIRS
Protector
of wild beasts.

PIXIES
often take
the form of
hedgehogs,
known in dialect
as urchins.

PIXIES

The Pixie, also variously known as Pisgie, piskie, pigsey, of Cornwall, is based in the district of Dartmoor.

> 'There's piskies up to Dartmoor
> And t'idden gude yu sez there bain't!'

There's hardly a place on Dartmoor that is not haunted by the green mischievous creatures. They have lent their name to many landmarks, Pixie's Holt, Pixie's Cave, Pixie's Parlour, Puggie Stone (the word Puggie has the same derivation as Puck). They dance in the shadows of the standing stones, or gambol on the tumbling stream edges. Their bells can be heard deep in the heart of the many tors on the moor.

> If thou'rt of air let grey mist fold thee,
> if of earth let the swart mine hold thee,
> if a Pixie sink thy ring*
> if a Nixie seek thy spring.
>
> WALTER SCOTT

The mischievous Pixies delight in stealing horses and Dartmoor ponies at night to ride them wildly across the moor, twisting and knotting their manes to spur them on. Even in the house one is not safe from them, for they like to throw pots and pans after the kitchen girls.

Although they enjoy their fun, the Pixies can be hard-working and often thresh corn at night for rewards of bread and cheese. However, one grateful farmer observing that the Pixie who threshed his corn wore clothes in tatters, got his wife to make up a tiny suit. This was left where the Pixie might find it at the beginning of his night's work. The Pixie, on seeing the brand new outfit, delightedly put it on, the threshing forgotten, and cried

> 'New Coat, New Waist-coat,
> New Breeches!
> You proud, I proud,
> I shan't work any more!'

Nor did he, leaving the farmer regretful of his kindness.

*faerie ring

to be misled by faeries,
whether by light or night,
or a subtle changing
of landmarks and features
by day, is described
as being
PIXY-LED

In Ireland this 'mis-leading' is attributed to a faerie tuft of grass or stray sod which when trodden on, triggers a spell. Under its influence, a usual experience when trying to cross a field is to discover that a stiled exit which may have been clearly visible on entering, has suddenly disappeared; and no amount of systematic searching of the surrounding hedges will reveal its whereabouts. In other cases a walker might abruptly find himself heading in a totally different direction to the way he wishes to go and no amount of re-alignment of his course seems to put this right. The spell may be counteracted by the traditional method of turning one's coat inside out and wearing it this way.

STRAY SOD
Anybody stepping on
a particular turf will
find himself unable
to continue his journey
even if he is in a
place well known
to him.

WILL O' THE WISP *In some remote areas*

a curious light resembling a flame is sometimes seen flickering in the distance. Traditionally known as ignis fatuus, this is also called Will o'the Wisp in the British Isles.

Although there are a number of theories on the nature of this phenomenon, no entirely satisfactory explanation has been put forward.

BOGIE is a generic name for a host of variously shaped goblins. Some are dangerous, some merely mischievous while others have shape-shifting powers.

PHOOKA

The Phooka is an Irish goblin with a variety of rough beast-like forms. He appears sometimes as a dog or a horse, or even a bull, but he is generally jet-black with blazing eyes. As a seemingly friendly, shaggy, sway-backed pony Phooka offers the unwary traveller a welcome lift; but once astride he is taken for a wild and terrifying gallop across the wettest and most thorny country, eventually to be dumped headlong into the mire or deposited in a ditch. The chuckle is that of the Phooka as he gallops away.

Phooka sometimes takes the form of an eagle and carries men on his back

PUCK
is, thanks to Shakespeare,
the most famous of the
mischievous shape-shifting
Hobgoblins.
He is closely related to
the Welsh Pwca and
the Irish Phooka.

On the
Shetland Islands
live the TROWS
These are similiar
to the Scandinavian
Trolls and, like them,
have an aversion
to daylight.
They are frequently
observed
performing a
curious lop-sided
dance called
'Henking

THE UNSEELIE COURT

The Scottish Unseelie Court, as opposed
to the more beneficient Seelie Court, are
thoroughly evil. While the Seelie court are
most commonly seen about twilight, the
Unseelie Court, or more particularly those
members
of it
known as
'The Host' fly
through the air at
night, snatching
up any mortals
unfortunate
enough to fall
in their
path.

The hapless
victims are dragged
along, beaten and
forced to participate in the
heinous activities of their
tormentors which include
throwing elf-shot at other
men and livestock

The Unseelie Court
also includes a great
variety of weird and
terrifying monstrosities.
These are usually
associated with particular
localities.

THE FACHAN
From the West Highlands of Scotland

The many HAGS
inhabiting the British Isles,
who seem to personify winter,
are probably survivals of the
oldest goddesses.

Some turn, like winter into
spring, from hideously ugly
old women into beautiful
young maidens, and others
like BLACK ANNIS
are cannibalistic.

BOGLES

are generally
evil-natured
Goblins although
they are
more disposed
to do harm to
liars and
murderers.

JACK-
IN-
IRONS
A
Yorkshire
giant who
haunts
lonely
roads

Despite his frightening
appearance
JIMMY SQUAREFOOT
is relatively harmless.

REDCAP is one of the most evil of the old Border Goblins. He lives in old ruined towers and castles, particularly those with a history of wickedness. He re-dyes his red cap in human blood.

The BEAN-NIGHE (Ben-Neeyah) or 'Washing
Woman' is the type of Banshee who haunts the lonely
streams of Scotland and Ireland, washing the
blood-stained garments of those about to die

It is said that these spirits are the ghosts of
women who died in childbirth and that they
are fated to perform their task until the day
when they would have normally died.

THE GREEN LADY OF CAERPHILLY

takes on the appearance of Ivy when she is not walking through the ruined castles she haunts

GWYLLION—

Welsh mountain fairies who have the disturbing habit of sitting amongst the rocks on either side of a mountain path and silently watching passing travelers.

LEANAN·SIDHE
(Lan-awn-shee)
On the Isle of Man
she is a blood-sucking
vampire and in Ireland
the muse of poets. Those
inspired by her live
brilliant, though short, lives.

THE KELPIE

is a Scottish water faerie. Although
sometimes appearing in the guise of a hairy man,
this is more often seen in the form of a young horse.
The Kelpie haunts rivers and streams and, after
letting unsuspecting humans mount him, will dash
into the water and give them a ducking.

The Each-Uisge (Ech-ooshkya), or Aughisky
(Agh-iski) as he is known in Ireland, inhabits seas
and lochs and is far more dangerous. After carrying
his victims into the water, he will tear them to
pieces and devour them, leaving nothing but the
liver.

If the Aughisky is ridden inland, he is quite safe, but
the slightest smell or sight of sea water will spell
death to the rider . . .

NUCKELAVEE

is surely the most awful of the Scottish
sea faeries. A monstrous horse with legs
that are part flipper, a huge mouth and
one fiery eye and, rising from its back,
joined to it at the waist, a hideous torso
with arms that nearly reach the ground,
topped by a massive head that rolls from
side to side as though its neck was too
weak to hold it upright.

Worse than this though is the horrible
appearance of the creature's flesh,
for it has no skin. Black blood coursing
through yellow veins, white sinews and
powerful red muscles are all exposed
to view.

The Nuckelavee has an aversion to fresh
running water and the pursued have
only to cross it to escape.

The WATER LEAPER
preys on Welsh
fishermen.

WATER FAERIES

Water has always
been of importance
in faerielore.
Its ambivalent nature
as provider of food,
nourisher of crops
and taker of lives makes
the divinities
associated with it
particularly potent.
   Like the rivers and
pools they inhabit,
the Glaistigs, Undines
Nixies, Lorelei,
Rusalki, Naiades and
others combine the qualities
of beauty
and treachery.

Those beings who dwell in or near rivers and streams tend to be less dangerous than their counterparts in the seas and lakes.

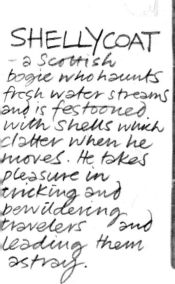

SHELLYCOAT

— a Scottish bogie who haunts fresh water streams and is festooned with shells which clatter when he moves. He takes pleasure in tricking and bewildering travelers and leading them astray.

URISK is
a Scottish solitary
faerie who haunts
lonely pools. He will
often seek out
human company
but his peculiar
appearance terrifies
those he approaches.

THE GLAISTIG

THE GLAISTIG is a water faerie and is part seductive woman, part goat. The goat-like attributes she tries to hide under a long flowing green dress. The Glaistig lures men to dance with her before she feeds, vampire-like, on their blood. Her nature is typically faerie-perverse - for she can also be benign and gently tend children or old people. She will also sometimes herd cattle for farmers.

PEG POWLER

JENNY GREENTEETH

There are many water spirits whose sole delight is the drowning and devouring of children. Probably most of these were invented by mothers to keep their children away from open river banks. The River Tees has one by the name of Peg Powler and a Yorkshire river is tenanted by Jenny Greenteeth. Both are green hags with long flowing hair and sharp teeth who drag their victims down to watery graves.

The ASRAI are
small and delicate
female faeries who
melt away
into a
pool of water
when captured or exposed to sunlight.

SELKIES

The seas around Orkney and Shetland
harbor the shy **Selkies** or Seal-Faeries
(known as the Roane in Ireland).
A female Selkie is able to discard her seal
skin and come ashore as a beautiful maiden.
If a human can capture this skin,
the Selkie can be forced to become a fine,
if wistful, wife. However, should she
ever find her skin she immediately
returns to the sea, leaving the husband
to pine and die. The males raise storms
and upturn boats to avenge the
indiscriminate slaughter of seals.

LUTEY AND THE MERMAID

In the old days the fishermen of Cornwall used to comb the seawrack on the beaches for valuables washed ashore from the many wrecks that were the toll of that cruelly rocky coast. One day Lutey of Cury, which is near Lizard Point, discovered a lovely mermaid stranded in one of the many tidepools to be found among the rocks.

She was a very beautiful creature and easily persuaded Lutey to carry her down to the receding sea. Snuggling against him, she offered him three wishes for his kindness and Lutey, who was a good man, chose first to have the power to break witchspells, second the power to force witch's familiars to do good to others, and third, that these two powers be inherited by his descendants.

The mermaid gladly granted these wishes and, because he had chosen wisely and unselfishly, she added two gifts – first, that none of his family should ever want, and second, a way for him to call her when needed by the use of her magic comb. He thanked her gravely and, still carrying her without effort, paced on toward the sea.

Now Lutey was a handsome man, and strong. And the mermaid began to wish that she might see more of him. She was a very lovely creature indeed, her silky, pale hair having a silvery cast to it, wide green eyes and a throaty liquid voice of great sweetness. When at last they came to the edge of the sea she began to plead with him to come into the water a little further, holding him tight about the neck when he would have put her down. Her voice was so gentle and the movement of her lithe body so sweet in his arms that Lutey strode on into the sea and would have been forever lost had not his dog barked frantically from the shore and reminded him of his own dear wife and children. But now the mermaid clung even more fiercely and would have dragged him down into the heavy sea until finally Lutey unsheathed his knife and threatened her with it.

The knife was of iron, a metal which is repulsive to merfolk, and she dashed away into the sea, calling as she went:

> 'Farewell, farewell!
> And keep thee well, my love!
> For nine long years I'll wait for thee
> And hold thee in my heart, my love
> And then I shall return!'

Lutey's wishes all came true and his family and descendants became famous healers. But the

MERMAIDS entice human lovers with their songs of enchantment. They cause ship-wrecking storms and are most frequently seen combing their long hair whilst admiring themselves in mirrors.

mermaid's promise also came true, for nine years to the day from the time when Lutey had cast her off she returned. He was out fishing with one of his sons, and she rose high in the water that was as green as her liquid eyes and shook her silky head and beckoned. Lutey turned to his son and said, 'It is time. I must pay my debt'. But he did not seem in the least unhappy as he leapt into the green depths with his silver-voiced love.

It is said also that ever after, every nine years, a Lutey of Cury would be lost to the sea. But whether they went as joyfully as the first Lutey no one knows.

MERROWS

The Irish merpeople are called Merrows and they can be distinguished from other sea-dwelling faeries in that they wear red feather caps to propel themselves down to their homes in the depths. Should their caps be stolen, they can no longer return to their watery homes. The female MERROWS are very beautiful and, like other Mermaids, appear before storms as an omen, but they are gentle by nature and often fall in love with mortal fishermen. This can partly be explained by the extreme ugliness of the male Merrows. Despite their alarming aspect, the males too have their redeeming features as they are generally amiable and jovial in character. Both males and females sometimes come ashore in the form of little hornless cattle.

THE BROWNIE is

called a variety of names according to location, i.e. Bwca (Booka) in Wales, Bodach in the Highlands, Fenoderee on the Isle of Man ; he has a number of characteristics which make him easily recognizable. Typically he is a small and shaggy man, wrinkled and brown in appearance, standing some twenty-five inches in height and either naked or dressed in tattered brown clothes. Whilst Highland Brownies have no fingers or toes, Lowland Brownies have no noses.

The Brownie generally 'adopts' a house which he then looks after. He has a very developed sense of responsibility and will come out at night to watch over farm animals, reap, thresh, mow, run errands and generally make himself indispensable. He will willingly do the work left undone by the servants although, should he feel they merit it, he will also plague them for their idleness. In Scotland, the Brownies help with the brewing.

For all his labors, however, the Brownie expects no more than a bowl of cream or best milk and a cake smeared with honey. Indeed, anything more and he will take offence and leave as has so often been the case when a kind-hearted householder has misguidedly left him the gift of fine clothes:

> 'What have we here, Hempen, Hampen!
> Here will I never more tread nor stampen.

Curiously though, there is at least one reported occasion of the Brownie taking umbrage because he esteemed the quality of a set of clothes left out for him to be inferior. . .

> 'Harden, harden, harden hamp!
> I will neither grind nor stamp,
> Had you given me linen gear,
> I had served you many a year,
> Thrift may go, bad luck may stay,
> I shall travel far away.'

Of course Brownies, like all faeries, are unpredictable in their behaviour and certainly one must take care not to offend them for, as already mentioned, the transition from helpful Brownie to troublesome Boggart is easily made. One Brownie whose mowing was criticized, had his revenge by throwing the entire harvest over a steep rock-face.

THE BWCA (Booka)

is the Welsh variety of Brownie. He will willingly churn butter if the kitchen and fireplace have been swept clean and a bowl of cream set next to the lighted fire. If mistreated or insulted, the Bwca will lose his temper and refuse to work. He will bang on the wall, throw things and even people through the air, pinch sleepers, destroy clothes, tell secrets out loud, howl and beat his tormentors. The householder should protect himself with iron, Holy water or crosses made from Mountain Ash. Then a Wise Man should be called in to banish the Bwca.

The Bwca despises teetotallers and people with long noses. One Welsh Brownie tormented a Baptist preacher who strongly disapproved of alcohol by jerking his stool away from him whilst he was praying, causing the unfortunate man to fall flat on his face, jangling the fire irons on the hearth, making dogs howl, frightening farmboys and maids and terrifying the preacher by taking his likeness. Finally the preacher fled with the Bwca riding pillion on his horse and grinning from ear to ear.

A Bwca on a Monmouthshire farm was tricked by a servant who left stale urine in a bowl for him instead of cream. He attacked her and then went to work at another farm where a curious girl wished to know his name but he refused to tell her. One evening all the men were out and the girl pretended to go out but crept to the foot of the stairs and heard him singing; 'How would she laugh, did she know that Gwarwyn-a-throt is my name'. She called out that she knew his name so he left and moved to a neighbouring farmhouse where he became friends with the manservant, Moses. Eventually Moses was killed at Bosworth field and Gwarwyn-a-throt turned bad and became so troublesome that a wise man was called in to 'lay' him. He got the Bwca to stick his long nose out of the hole where he was hiding and transfixed it with an awl; the Bwca was swept away in a whirlwind to the Red Sea.

THE FENODEREE

A type of brownie from the Isle of Man. A willing
worker of prodigious strength, the Fenoderee
performs many labours for the farmers of Man. His
strength and enthusiasm are not matched by his
intelligence however and this was evident when he
rounded up a hare with the flock of sheep in his
charge. There was also an occasion when he was
tricked into trying to fetch water in a sieve.

The Fenoderee was a member of the
Ferrishyn – the faerie tribe of Man,
until he made the mistake of absenting
himself from their Autumn festival to
court a mortal girl. His good looks were
taken from him and he became the
solitary, ugly creature he is now.

Like the
Brownies
he is greatly
offended by the
offer of clothes
and will
leave his
employment.

He is a famous mower
noted for
his thoroughness.

The
KILLMOULIS
is a particularly
ugly Brownie
who haunts mills.
He is characterized by
an enormous nose and no
mouth.
To eat he presumably stuffs
the food up his nose.
Although a Killmoulis works
hard for the miller, he
delights in practical jokes
and can therefore be a
hindrance rather than
a help.

FINCASTLE MILL

One of the best-known of the Highland Brownies is Meg or Maggy Moulach. Meg had a son, Brownie-Clod, who however was a Dobie, a rather stupid variety of Brownie. One tale tells of a certain Fincastle Mill that was reputed to be haunted so no-one dared set foot there after dark. One night however, a girl who was making a cake for her wedding discovered she had run short of meal. Finding no-one willing to go to the mill for her, she had to go herself. She made up a big fire, put a pot of water on to boil and began to grind the meal. On the dot of midnight, an ugly little brown man came into the mill, edged towards her and when she asked who he was, replied by asking her what her name was. She answered: 'Oh, I'm Mise mi fein' (me myself). The Brownie edged closer to her leering in an unpleasant manner until she took fright and poured a ladle of boiling water over him. At this he screeched in anger and flew at her. She defended herself by pouring the rest of the boiling water over him. He fled out of the door, mortally burned,

to Maggy Mouloch, who asked him who was responsible for hurting him in that way – he replied that it was 'Me myself.'

But the girl did not escape Maggy's wrath for long. Some time later when she was married she was asked to tell a story so she recounted how she had tricked the Brownie at Fincastle Mill. Unbeknown to her Maggy Mouloch was outside and heard every word and she had her revenge immediately, throwing a three-legged stool so violently at the young bride that she was killed on the spot.

Maggy Mouloch then found a new home near a farm where the servants paid her with bread and cream for her help. She worked so conscientiously however that the farmer decided to dismiss all the servants and rely on her work. She retaliated by going on strike and becoming a full-time Boggart, plaguing him so much that he was forced to rehire the rest of the servants.

FAERIE FLORA

The FOXGLOVE derives its name from 'Little Folks-glove', for the florets are worn by faeries, sometimes as hats, sometimes as gloves. Another name often attributed to the flower is 'Goblin's Thimbles'! Not, perhaps, inapt, considering that the Foxglove contains digitalis, a heart stimulant and source of wild, dark excitement that Goblins bring.

'Swift fire spread through her veins, knocked at her heart...'

GOBLIN MARKET
Christina Rossetti

HAREBELL

PRIMROSES boast a unique power - they make the invisible visible and to eat them is a sure way to see faeries. If one touches a faerie rock with the correct number of Primroses in a posy, the way is opened to faerieland and faerie gifts, but the wrong number opens the door to doom.

RAGWORT

and Rye-grass are used
by faeries as make-shift
horses. John Aubrey
in the 17th century
states that 'Horse and
Hattock' were the
magic words to make
the stems fly.

WILD THYME

Bees, which are considered to be messengers of the Gods, have a particular fondness for this blossom. 'To see the Fayries' a brew must be concocted including Wild Thyme 'the tops of which must be gathered near the side of a hill where the fayries use to be oft, and the grass of a fayrie throne.'

Like other flowers that are the favorites of Faerie, Wild Thyme is dangerous to bring into the house.

COWSLIPS

Flowers have always been an intertwined link between the human world and Faerie and are the special charge of the faeries. Cowslips in particular are loved and guarded by faeries. These are distinguished by their power to find hidden faerie gold and are also known as 'Culver's Keys' (keys to unlock the way to treasure) in the West of England.

Where the bee sucks there suck I,
In a cowslip's bell I lie. ARIEL

Act V The Tempest
William Shakespeare

THE PANSY
is the 'little western flower' that was used as a love potion by Oberon.

The Pansy that grew in Elizabethan England was the little Viola tricolor, loved equally by the common man and by Faerie. It had many country names such as 'Tickle my Fancy', 'Pink of my John', 'Three faces under a hood', 'Love in Idleness' but 'Heart's Ease' was the most common.

Another popular flower which is filled
with danger is the BLUEBELL. The Scottish name
for the plant is 'Deadmen's Bells' for to hear the ring
of a Bluebell is to hear one's death knell, The Bluebell
is one of the most potent of all faerie flowers, and a
bluebell wood is an extremely hazardous place to be —
a place of faerie-woven spells and enchantments

The four leaf
CLOVER will
break a faerie spell.

ST. JOHN'S WORT is even more efficacious against spells for it provides actual protection from faeries. The St. John's Wort, being a sun symbol like the daisy, was used extensively in Midsummer pagan festivals, and is both a powerful protection and a healing plant.

FAERIE TREES

Many trees are the haunts of Faerie. Humans foolish enough to pass by a host-tree late at night find their arms bruised or pinched by small faerie fingers. Three Thorn trees growing closely together at an acute angle are especially potent and should be approached warily if at all. Or on the other hand, Thorn tree branches can be hung with ribbons and even rags as propitiating gifts for the faeries.

Other trees most favoured by the faeries are the Blackthorn, Hazel, Alder, Elder and Oak. Elementals and strange creatures haunt these trees, especially if twisted together; two Thorns and an Elder are thought to be a particularly dangerous combination. So are Oak, Ash and Thorn. Strangely, however, a twig from each bound together with red thread is a protective charm against evil and hostile spirits.

In general, however, one should beware faerie trees for they are fiercely protected. As with all things faerie, one must approach the benefits with caution.

In Celtic
legend the HAZEL
nut was the receptacle of knowledge
Additionally, in England, the hazelnut
has always been a fertility symbol.

WHITETHORN

The ROWAN tree is also considered effective against bad spirits:
  'Rowan tree, red thraid,
   Puts the Witches to their speed!'

Rowan wood was used
to make butter
churns to
ensure the
butter was not
'overlooked' by faeries
or witches. Bewitched
horses can always be
controlled by a Rowan whip.

The 'Flying Rowan' - that
is, a tree growing with its
roots not in the ground.
(in a cleft in a rock, or in
the branches of another tree)
is considered the most
efficacious.

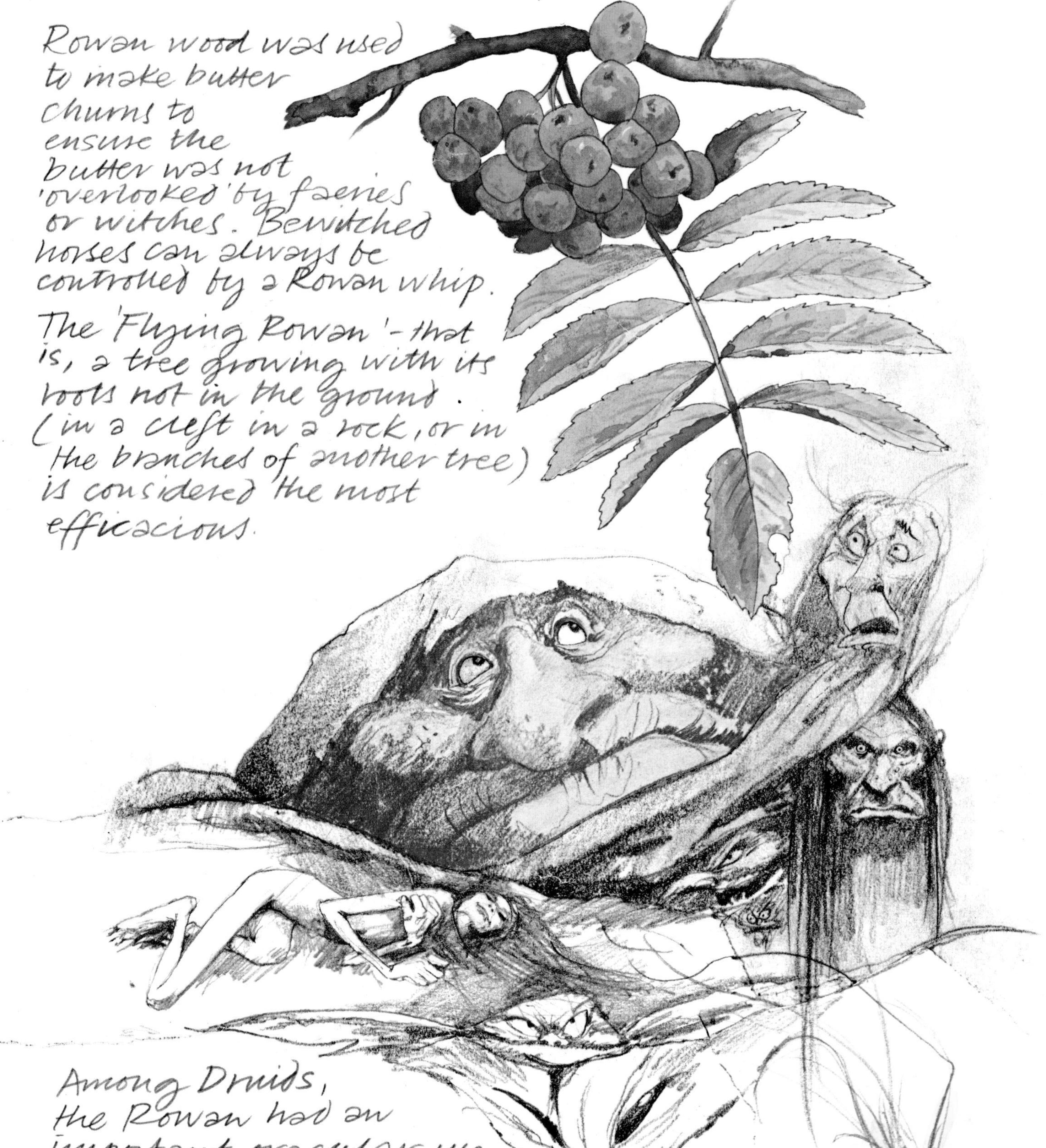

Among Druids,
the Rowan had an
important oracular use.
Fires of the wood were used
to conjure up spirits who
could be forced to answer
Questions when Rowanberries
were spread on the newly flayed hides
of bulls.

LUNANTISHEE

Guardians
of
Blackthorn
trees

'Fairy Folkes Are in old Oakes!'

A felled oak will send up shoots
from the stump, forming a coppice haunted
by the Oakmen, angry at the loss
of their parent tree. Food offered by
Oakmen to passing mortals may seem
irresistibly tempting but one should
beware for it is nothing but poisonous
fungi, disguised by 'Glamour.'

'Ellum do grieve,
Oak he do hate
Willow do walk
If Yew travels late'

WILLOW trees actually
uproot themselves at night and
and stalk muttering behind unwary travelers.

The ELDER tree is sometimes a witch
in tree form, and should not be axed
without asking her leave :
'Ourd gal, give me of thy wood
An Oi will give some of moine
When Oi grows inter a tree :

Children should never
be laid in an elderwood
cradle, for the faeries will
pinch them black and blue,
while to burn Elder logs is to
invite disaster as these bring
the Devil into the house.

The spirit of the BIRCH tree is called
'The One with the White Hand'.
If the hand touches a head it leaves a vivid
white mark and inflicts madness, but if
it touches a heart it is the touch of death.

The ALDER tree is protected
by water spirits.

The last apple of
the year's crop
should be left
for the 'Apple-Tree-Man'
to ensure
future good harvests

ASH

Druids' wands were made of Ash twigs and, moreover, the Ash has healing properties. In early homeopathic practice, weak-limbed children were passed through split Ash trees which were then bound up. If the tree grew again soundly, so would the child.

TOADSTOOLS

There are many folktales and songs linking the people of the hills' with toadstools whose sudden appearance and rapid growth have always seemed uncanny to man. Hence some supernatural agency must be their cause. The European St Veit, on 15th June, rides through the woods on his blind horse sowing toadstools. Their unearthly shapes and colors (sometimes even luminous) and their often poisonous nature are considered a sure sign that these growths are the Devil's or faerie spawn:

> . . . you whose pastime
> Is to make midnight mushrooms.

The toadstool most associated with faerie is the red Fly Agaric (Amarita Muscovia). This is a toadstool with poisonous hallucinogenic properties. The Vikings ate this magic fungus to gain their fighting frenzy known as 'Berserk'.

In viking mythology Woton was once chased by devils and the red flecks of foam falling from the mouth of his galloping, six-limbed steed, Slepnir, were magically transformed into red toadstools. Fly Agaric was thus a gift from the Gods. The Celts had a taboo on the red toadstools and, indeed, on many red foods like rowan berries and red nuts and fruits. These were the food of the Gods.

Similarly Robert Graves considers that Amarita Muscovia is in fact the nectar and ambrosia of the Greek Gods, a statement that is reinforced by similar attribution and use of the sacred mushrooms by peoples as far apart as Siberia, Mexico and Borneo. Extracts from the Fly Agaric induce in the partakers great animation during which they dance wildly, have visions and talk to invisible people. What better mushroom to be a magic faerie seat or a gateway to faerieland.

Faerie has claimed many toadstools as its particular property as reflected in names such as Yellow Fairy Club, Slender Elf Cap, Dune Pixie-Hood and Dryad's Saddle.

Despite the name,
the Elf-Cap Toadstools
are not worn by the
elves as hats — they prefer
a more elaborate
style.

Gregarious
Elf-Cap

The 'FAIRY RING MUSHROOM' is the one which marks the boundary of the faeries favorite dancing places.
The Rings themselves have been proved by modern science to be often of great antiquity, some being over 600 years old.

FAERIE ENCOUNTERS

At the time of the English Civil War there lived a certain Anne Jefferies who became quite notorious for her claims of having been carried away by the little people, her powers of clairvoyance and healing by touch.

Anne recounted that she was knitting one day in a shady nook when she heard a rustling. Believing this to be her sweetheart she decided to pretend she had heard nothing. Then she heard a suppressed laugh and a tinkling sound and six handsome little men dressed in green came into the arbor. One of them, the finest of all, had a red feather in his cap. He spoke to her lovingly and, when she put out her hand to him, jumped onto her palm. When Anne set the faerie down on her lap, he clambered up her bosom and began to kiss her neck. She was enchanted with his love-making. The other five little men then climbed on her dress and smothered her with kisses.

Suddenly one touched her eyes, she was plunged into darkness and felt herself transported through the air. She was set down, opened her eyes and found herself in a wondrous land of lush trees, beautiful flowers, gold and silver palaces, lakes of glittering fish and brilliantly colored song birds. Magnificently clad people were promenading, resting, dancing or indulging in pastimes. They now seemed no smaller than Anne who found herself garbed in the same fine manner as they. Blissfully happy, courted by her six friends, Anne could have stayed there forever.

Later she stole away with her beau with the red feather but the five others, with an angry crowd in their wake, broke in on their happiness. Again she was plunged into darkness, whisked into the air and finally found herself on the floor of her arbor surrounded by worried friends.

Although Anne continued to be guarded by the faeries who nourished her with faerie food, as people came to see her from far and wide and her fame spread she was persecuted by the Authorities, arrested in 1646 and committed to prison. She was not fed but thrived on faerie victuals. Eventually she was released but, understandably, would speak no more of her visit to the realm.

Theosophy recognises the world of Faerie as a part
of a usually hidden spiritual world that co-exists
with our physical world. In the theosophists' view
the general function of faeries is to absorb PRANA
or vitality from the sun and distribute this to the
physical. Thus the flower faeries are nature spirits for
they provide the vital link between the sun's energy
and the soil's minerals. Certain faeries are
responsible for the structure and color of flowers;
others work below ground around the roots; others
on a molecular level are concerned with cell growth.
Still other faerie species aid the development of the
mineral, vegetable, and animal kingdom.

The faerie body comprises the finest states of physical matter. When faeries are visible they are on an ETHERIC level (a state more subtle than gaseous) and when invisible they are on an ASTRAL level (a state even finer than etheric). They are able to change levels at will, but on the finer levels are only visible to the clairvoyant. The matter of their form is so sensitive and fluid that it can be molded by such tenuous things as thought and feeling. Their normal state is a pulsating sphere of light with a bright nucleus, but when this condenses and they materialise on the etheric level, they often use a collective consciousness as a blueprint for their form. In this way form is determined by imitating elements of plants and animals, or by using a traditional mold; or by intercepting human sub-conscious thought patterns.

Thus a faerie's appearance will often reflect our own preconceptions of faeries. Not unnaturally faerie forms are both numerous and varied, but are generally based on a diminutive human figure with, usually, some defect or exaggeration of feature or limb. Because of the nature of its etheric structure a faerie can change its size at will but, if naturally small, to maintain a larger size for any period of time is a considerable strain. In order to take on a new form a faerie must conceive it clearly and keep it fixed firmly in its consciousness, for as soon as the thought waivers its form reverts back to normal. The energies that flow through the faerie body often help to create flowing hair and outspread wings of brilliant, ever-changing hues. These pinions are not used for flight for faeries can travel through air and matter at will.

Common experience and clairvoyant sightings of faeries prove that the faeries of tradition are the faeries of fact. Clairvoyant Geoffrey Hodson in his book *Fairies at Work and at Play* describes his faerie sightings:

The Household Brownie that lived in Mr. Hodson's house was:

> . . . some five or six inches high, wears a conical brown cap, of a texture like deerskin, tilted at the back of his head. He has a bright, youthful clean-shaven countenance, with fresh colour, and dark brown eyes which are round and bright. The neck is a little too long and thin for our sense of proportion. He is clothed in a green, close-fitting coatee; knee-breeches, and brownish-grey stockings of a rough material; at the present moment he is wearing large boots somewhat out of proportion to the rest of his body.

A Golden Fairy – she is decidedly fair in colouring, full of laughter and happiness, very open and fearless in expression, and is surrounded by an aura of golden radiance in which the outline of her wings can be traced. There is also a hint of mockery in her attitude and expression, as of one who is enjoying a joke against the poor mortals who are studying her.

In a waterfall he sees an Undine:

> . . . in the form of a full-sized nude female of singular beauty. The hair is fair and shining, the brow broad, the features beautifully modelled, the eyes large and luminous and, while their expression has something of the spirit of the wilds, their glance is not unkindly.

In Epping Forest he describes tree spirits as green with the appearance:

> . . . of young girls, and are of human height. They have long dark hair which hangs loose and gives them a rather wild look. Some are wearing garlands and loosely hanging necklaces of leaves . . .

Wood Elves are tiny and:

. . . appeared as if completely covered in a tight fitting one-piece skin, which shone as if wet, and was coloured like the bark of a tree. Their hands and feet were large, out of all proportion to the rest of their bodies. Their legs were thin, and their ears ran upwards to a point. Their noses too were pointed and their mouths were wide.

THOMAS THE RHYMER, a XIIIth century poet, experienced the enchantment of Faerie. One day, as he lay down on Huntlie bank, no less a person than the Queen of Elfland, dressed in green, rode past on a horse whose mane was praised with countless silver faerie bells.

He was trapped by a kiss and taken on the back of the horse across deserts and rivers of blood to a green garden in Elfland.

An apple gave him the gift of prophecy and a tongue that could not lie.

True Thomas lay oer yond grassy bank,
And he beheld a ladie gay,
A ladie that was brisk and bold,
Come riding oer the fernie brae.

Her skirt was of the grass-green silk,
Her mantel of the velvet fine,
At ilka tett of her horse's mane
Hung fifty silver bells and nine.

True Thomas he took off his hat,
And bowed him low down till his knee:
'All hail, thou mighty Queen of Heaven!
For your peer on earth I never did see.'

'O no, O no, True Thomas,' she says,
'That name does not belong to me;
I am but the queen of fair Elfland,
And I'm come here for to visit thee.

'But ye maun go wi me now, Thomas,
True Thomas, ye maun go wi me,
For ye maun serve me seven years,
Thro weel or wae as may chance to be.'

She turned about her milk-white steed,
And took True Thomas up behind,
And aye wheneer her bridle rang,
The steed flew swifter in the wind.

For forty days and forty nights
He wade thro red blude to the knee,
And he saw neither sun nor moon,
But heard the roaring of the sea.

O they rade on, and further on,
Until they came to a garden green:
'Light down, light down, ye ladie free,
Some of that fruit let me pull to thee.'

'O no, O no, True Thomas,' she says,
'That fruit maun not be touched by thee,
For a' the plagues that are in hell
Light on the fruit of this countrie.

'But I have a loaf here in my lap,
Likewise a bottle of claret wine,
And now ere we go farther on,
We'll rest a while, and ye may dine.'

When he had eaten and drunk his fill,
'Lay down your head upon my knee,'
The lady sayd, 'ere we climb yon hill,
And I will show you fairlies three.

'O see not ye yon narrow road,
So thick beset wi thorns and briers?
That is the path of righteousness,
Tho after it but few enquires.

'And see not ye that braid braid road,
That lies across yon lillie leven?
That is the path of wickedness,
Tho some call it the road to heaven.

'And see not ye that bonny road,
Which winds about the fernie brae?
That is the road to fair Elfland,
Whe(re) you and I this night maun gae.

'But Thomas, ye maun hold your tongue,
Whatever you may hear or see,
For gin ae word you should chance to speak,
You will neer get back to your ain countrie.'

He has gotten a coat of the even cloth,
And a pair of shoes of velvet green,
And till seven years were past and gone
True Thomas on earth was never seen.

The English and Scottish Popular Ballads
FRANCIS JAMES CHILD

Thomas lived for seven years in Elfland before he
returned to earth to write poetry and make true
prophecies. Some say that eventually he went back
and still lives on as an adviser in the faerie court.
But others never return from the land of Faerie.
Among these there are the handsome lads lured away to
become the lovers of faerie princesses, and the young boys
who are given work to do or those who are trained as
extra soldiers for faerie battles.

TAM LIN

Janet has kilted her green kirtle
A little aboon her knee,
And she has snooded her yellow hair
A little aboon her bree,
And she is to her father's ha,
As fast as she can hie.

Four and twenty ladies fair
Were playing at the ba,
And out then cam the fair Janet,
Ance the flower amang them a'.

Four and twenty ladies fair
Were playing at the chess,
And out then cam the fair Janet,
As green as onie glass.

Out then spak an auld grey knight,
Lay oer the castle wa,
And says, Alas, fair Janet, for thee
But we'll be blamed a'.

'Haud your tongue, ye auld fac'd knight,
Some ill death may ye die!
Father my bairn on whom I will,
I'll father nane on thee.'

Out then spak her father dear,
And he spak meek and mild;
'And ever alas, sweet Janet,' he says,
'I think thou gaes wi child.'

'If that I gae wi child, father,
Mysel maun bear the blame;
There's neer a laird about your ha
Shall get the bairn's name.

'If my love were an earthly knight,
As he's an elfin grey,
I wad na gie my ain true-love
For nae lord that ye hae.

'The steed that my true-love rides on·
Is lighter than the wind;
Wi siller he is shod before,
Wi burning gowd behind.'

Janet has kilted her green kirtle
A little aboon her knee,
And she has snooded her yellow hair
A little aboon her bree,
And she's awa to Carterhaugh
As fast as she can hie.

When she cam to Carterhaugh,
Tam Lin was at the well,
And there she fand his steed standing,
But away was himsel.

She had na pu'd a double rose,
A rose but only twa,
Till up then started young Tam Lin,
Says Lady, thou pu's nae mae.

Why pu's thou the rose, Janet,
Amang the groves sae green,
And a' to kill the bonnie babe
That we gat us between?'

'O tell me, tell me, Tam Lin,' she says,
'For's sake that died on tree,
If eer ye was in holy chapel,
Or christendom did see?'

'Roxbrugh he was my grandfather,
Took me with him to bide,
And ance it fell upon a day
That wae did me betide.

'And ance it fell upon a day,
A cauld day and a snell,
When we were frae the hunting come
That frae my horse I fell;
The Queen o Fairies she caught me,
In yon green hill to dwell.

'And pleasant is the fairy land,
But, an eerie tale to tell,
Ay at the end of seven years
We pay a tiend to hell;
I am sae fair and fu o flesh,
I'm feard it be mysel.

'But the night is Halloween, lady,
The morn is Hallowday;
Then win me, win me, an ye will,
For weel I wat ye may.

'Just at the mirk and midnight hour
The fairy folk will ride,
And they that was their true-love win,
At Miles Cross they maun bide.'

'But how shall I thee ken, Tam Lin,
Or how my true-love know,
Amang sae mony unco knights,
The like I never saw?'

'O first let pass the black, lady,
And syne let pass the brown,
But quickly run to the milk-white steed,
Pu ye his rider down.

'For I'll ride on the milk-white steed,
And ay nearest the town;
Because I was an earthly knight
They gie me that renown.

'My right hand will be glovd, lady,
My left hand will be bare,
Cockt up shall my bonnet be,
And kaimd down shall be my hair,
And thae's the takens I gie thee,
Nae doubt I will be there.

'They'll turn me in your arms, lady,
Into an esk and adder;
But hold me fast, and fear me not,
I am your bairn's father.

'They'll turn me to a bear sae grim,
And then a lion bold;
But hold me fast, and fear me not,
As ye shall love your child.

'Again they'll turn me in your arms
To a red het gaud of airn;
But hold me fast, and fear me not,
I'll do to you nae harm.

'And last they'll turn me in your arms
Into the burning gleed;
Then throw me into well water,
O throw me in wi speed.

'And then I'll be your ain true-love,
I'll turn a naked knight;
Then cover me wi your green mantle,
And cover me out o sight.'

Gloomy, gloomy was the night,
And eerie was the way,
As fair Jenny in her green mantle
To Miles Cross she did gae.

About the middle o the night
She heard the bridles ring;
This lady was as glad at that
As any earthly thing.

First she let the black pass by,
And syne she let the brown;
But quickly she ran to the milk-white steed,
And pu'd the rider down.

Sae weel she minded whae he did say,
And young Tam Lin did win;
Syne coverd him wi her green mantle,
As blythe's a bird in spring.

Out then spak the Queen o Fairies,
Out of a bush o broom,
'Them that has gotten young Tam Lin
Has gotten a stately groom.'

Out then spak the Queen o Fairies,
And an angry woman was she:
'Shame betide her ill-far'd face,
And an ill death may she die,
For she's taen awa the bonniest knight
In a' my companie.

'But had I kend, Tam Lin,' she says,
'What now this night I see,
I wad hae taen out thy twa grey een,
And put in twa een o tree.'

The English and Scottish Popular Ballads
FRANCIS JAMES CHILD

While working on the illustrations for this book, Brian Froud received this unusual letter and drawing from Matawan, New Jersey...

Dec. 30, 1977

Dear Mr Froud,

      Please forgive this intrusion – it isn't my usual habit to annoy strangers with correspondence. However, I happen to be one of the great many admirers of your work and this is a sort of fan letter. Recently I inherited one of the oldest houses in New Jersey (1677) and it was necessary for me to clean the place out and sell it. Since it has been in the family since before the Revolution, this is rather a large and interesting project, if a trifle melancholy. I am a toymaker and a builder of horsedrawn wagons by profession and, though I love this work, it does not provide the sort of income necessary to maintain a large country house. (This is O.K. by me, however, as I really don't want to live here for a variety of reasons). One of my favorite items in the house is the enclosed sketch which I would be honored if you would accept as a token of my appreciation of many happy hours spent studying your drawings. The story behind the sketch is as follows; During the summer of 1887 my great grandfather, James M. Hawkins, cut down a dead apple-tree near the house. After the tree was down he got a book, a pipe and a mug of tea and went back outside to rest a bit. Shortly there appeared on a branch of the tree, an old man with a pin feather in his cap and a full white beard. He was about six inches tall but was otherwise unremarkable. They regarded each other for a while and the little man asked why he had cut down the tree. G. Grandfather replied that it was dead and would have fallen in the winter. The little man asked what he would do with it and was informed it would be fire wood. At this, the little man flew into a rage and said he had lived in the tree for years and wouldn't see his home casually burned and if G. Grandfather did so dispose of it he would suffer for it. G. Grandfather asked what he should do with it and the little man gave it some thought and replied he should make a cradle for his children and they would have good fortune. Thereupon he stamped a foot, said something in a "foreign" language which G. Grandfather said sounded like an Indian tongue and was gone. G. Grandfather at once took out a pencil and recorded the little man's likeness on the flyleaf of his book. He made the cradle, a really nice piece of work which I cherish and which impresses me very much, having tried to work apple wood myself with no success – very gnarly and grainy and hard to do anything with.

      His children did do rather well, all being successful and living to old age. For whatever it's worth, I might add that G. Grandfather was a man with a reputation for being quite dour and not given to fancies at all.

      You may or may not be aware that there are native legends in America regarding elves, sprites etc. The Leni-Lenapi Indians (the local tribe hereabouts) called them "Nan A Push" which literally means "little people of the forest".

      Anyway, it strikes me that items such as this sketch really only have value if they are passed around.........

                  Yours with best wishes,
                  Toby Grace.

*The following
pages constitute a
photographic record of an
expedition made by Messrs Froud
and Lee following completion of much
of the illustration for this book.*

*Their aim was to complement the material already gathered
with some up-to-date faerie sightings but, despite a thoroughly
researched itinerary covering known faerie haunts, they returned disappointed.*

*Subsequently the snapshots taken were submitted for minute examination
by a panel of experts who maintain that they do in fact show evidence of
faerie presence.*

A technical note

Over the many months during which the author/illustrators researched and compiled this volume, serious doubts arose over the authenticity of information pertaining to the existence, nature and rôle of 'Gnomes' in faerielore. The proper noun itself was probably born of a simple mistranslation combining the root of the Mediaeval Latin 'gnomus' and the Greek verb γνωρίζω (to know). Alternatively it has been suggested that 'Gnome' is derived from, or is even an erroneous elision of, the Greek γενομὸς which, comparable to the word θαλασσινὸς meaning 'of or from the sea', could conceivably have been understood to signify 'of the earth'.

At all events the resulting noun was probably used in reference to a breed of small people to be found in the remoter mountain regions of the Northern Hemisphere and notably the Carpathian mountains. These people used to mine the rock quarries of the mountains many centuries ago and hence popular legend could have described them as having actually inhabited the bowels of the earth rather in the manner of Dwarfs or Knockers. They were also said to be intimately acquainted with the locations of precious metals and stones, (hence the Greek root word indicating knowledge?).

Anthropologists, however, can see no foundation for suggestions that these people might not have belonged to our race. Archeological remains have included both human and animal bones, various receptacles in pottery and glass, metal tools, fragments of leather and fibre and also charred stones which are assumed to have been used in or around fires.

Elsewhere, a race of 'little people', ie small in stature, is also known to have inhabited the caves along the Mediterranean coast of Southern Spain. The existence of such cave-dwelling people might well also have given rise to stories of 'Gnomes'.

Possibly the most likely theory, however, is that the word 'Gnome' came to be used in the English language through the writings of the 16th-century Swiss alchemist, Paracelsus.

Paracelsus was variously regarded as wise man, magician and rogue but certainly the man himself had no doubts as to his capabilities for he called himself Paracelsus to proclaim his superiority over Aulus Cornelius Celsus, the celebrated author of *De Medicina*.

One of Paracelsus' works was entitled *Liber de nymphis, sylphis, pygmaeis et salamandris et caeteribus spiritibus* in which he propounds the theory of existence of four spiritual beings: the sylphs of the air, the salamanders of the fire, the nymphs of the water and the pygmies of the earth.

Writing in Latin, he also referred to the pygmies as 'gnomi' which has the singular 'gnomus'. Paracelsus' 'Gnomes' were able to move through the earth 'unobstructed as fish do through water, or birds and land animals through air.' However, whether he coined the word 'Gnome' himself or simply culled it from the writings of an earlier author is unknown.

The authors have concluded thus that the 'Gnomes' so familiarly met in popular folk and faerielore do not figure amongst the denizens of the Realm of Faerie. They do not, in fact, exist. The most feasible explanation for the abundance of so-called genuine faerie stories featuring 'Gnomes' is that they have resulted from the romantic elaborations of recent writers.

We regret that we have had to dismiss 'Gnomes' as such from this volume.

But we may be wrong . .